THEY ARE LIVING IN CHAINS

THEY ARE LIVING IN CHAINS

My Quest to Liberate Africa's "Untouchables"

BY GRÉGOIRE AHONGBONON

with the collaboration of Thomas Oswald

Translation by James Henri McMurtrie

SOPHIA INSTITUTE PRESS
Manchester, New Hampshire

Sophia Institute Press
Box 5284, Manchester, NH 03108
1-800-888-9344
www.SophiaInstitute.com

Sophia Institute Press is a registered trademark of Sophia Institute.

paperback ISBN 978-1-64413-702-4

ebook ISBN 978-1-64413-703-1

Library of Congress Control Number: 2022940882

First printing

CONTENTS

THEY ARE LIVING IN CHAINS

1

THE NAIL

I liked it when the drive went like this. There was traffic, of course, as always, but only enough to make it interesting. I was driving on Bouaké's main road in Côte d'Ivoire. There is no comparison with Europe's roads, which are so beautiful, smooth, and boring. Here, we must constantly adapt and analyze situations in a fraction of a second.

We were, naturally, driving on the left side, not on the right, as we inherited from the French. The right lane is generally less drivable. A crowd of street vendors was encroaching on it. They were selling gas, which comes from Nigeria and was dispensed in large glass bottles. The vendors were also selling fruits—pineapples, bananas, and papayas—which sometimes grow on the edge of the road. In addition to all the traffic, some broken-down cars rounded out this road's congestion. There were also animals: hens, goats, pigs, and sheep wandered on the roadsides and sometimes on the crossings. Those that were too daring were prey for roving dogs.

Two trucks with incredible loads were blocking the road in front of me. There was an unimpeded space with just a little yellowed grass on the right side of the second truck, and the ground looked safe to drive on. I could try to pass them. A motorcycle cruised in front of me. I tailgated it and blew my horn. The driver let me go by, and I passed it under the nonchalant gaze of workers who were resting on a pile of burlap bags from the truck on the right. The maneuver lasted less than five seconds. I could leisurely make the engine roar in the available space in front of me—for a while, at least —before the next obstacle.

I headed up a taxi company. Even before I worked in this business, I had the reputation of being a fast driver. I myself drove one of the five cabs in my little fleet. I did this in order not to lose time but also because I had noticed that I earned four times more than my employees. I, of course, was good at this job. I went fast and didn't have many accidents. But my "friends" were obviously into the till or lazing around. When I came back with my daily groceries, I had a little more money and, above all, a good argument to put a bit more pressure on my employees. People are like cars. They wear out. You have to replenish them regularly and make sure everything is running well!

I must admit that I didn't give a lot of time to my employees or my family. My wife, Léontine, and my two children didn't see me much. They never blamed me for it. They saw how I worked. Every franc was reinvested. Every item was used again. I started my job repairing tires. Here in Africa, when a tire goes flat, it isn't replaced. We fill the holes and use it again—all the way to the layer of its base. I gave my family and my employees enough attention, nevertheless.

At the present, since I didn't have any clients, I took advantage of the down time to stop off at the fish shop, where I bought the most beautiful St. Pierre fish on the plank. From the seat next to me, it looked at me with its big eye. The day was coming to an end, and this time, I had a client in the back, who whistled admiringly when he saw my "catch."

"Say, I didn't think a taxi driver could buy an animal like that one! I think I'm going to change jobs!"

"It's because I'm not a taxi driver. I'm the boss!" I laughed when I answered him.

"So, if you're the boss, you must be able to take me to City Hall in ten minutes, right? I'm late!"

I looked at him in the rearview mirror with a hint of malice. The man was big and fat. He was wearing one of those three-piece suits that you inflict on yourself here as a sign of success, despite the heat. He was certainly an important person — or one who wanted to seem important.

I stepped on the accelerator. The late-day traffic ground to a halt at a red light. I took advantage of a large sidewalk to throw off guard the line of motorcycles and trucks waiting for the green light. I knew the corner and all the tricks. I slid into it, avoided a wandering goat, and went full speed ahead on an unpaved crossroad that was drivable in this dry season. My client was delighted with my performance and commented: "That's good! Bravo!" — while periodically drying the sweat on his forehead and his neck, which sported a tie.

I was thrilled about my performance. I was thinking that the guy would leave me a generous tip, which I didn't need. But it was a small victory. It was a beautiful drive to complete a very full day. The path got narrower. The neophyte would think it would end in a cul-de-sac. But, in fact, it was a passage to the main road. I hastily got on the congested road and took advantage of a narrow passage in the traffic — before brutally jamming on the brakes. A completely naked man was crossing in front of me. I noticed that his right eye was missing. He was running without heeding the vehicles or horns. A truck slammed on its brakes with difficulty and almost ran him down. In fact, I had the fleeting impression that this lunatic wanted someone to run him down. That being said, I didn't have time to think about it anymore.

"Oh! The fish fell!"

My client in the back was complaining about my beautiful St. Pierre fish, which has fallen off the passenger seat because of my braking action. I delicately picked it up and put it back in its place. Then I drove on. The naked man had disappeared. Nobody had "picked him up."

We arrived at City Hall in a timely fashion, and my client thanked me. Yet I had an odd impression of something that would ruin the perfect day of a businessman who was always on the go: on my way home, the car careened. When I got home, I had to face reality: my brand-new tire, which I had just changed, was flat. But I immediately found out where the problem was, thanks to my experience as a repairman. I had driven over a machine screw with my brand-new tire. The damage was minor. One of my employees would repair this in an hour tomorrow.

Yet this annoyed me. It left me with the feeling that a bad spell had been cast on the day.

This was nonsense. I had never believed in bad luck or witches, unlike my compatriots from Benin. I believed in work and success. Despite this little "nail" in my day, I had filled my day well, and I even returned home in time for dinner.

Léontine welcomed the St. Pierre fish with a smile and left her pots and pans. She had already planned a meal in case, as usual, I came home late. But she started to scale the monster without any criticism.

Soon, all four of us were around the table. My oldest child, Bruno, was only five. But he was demanding an enormous slice of fish. His younger brother, Moïse -Florent, tasted a little piece, which he chewed with an inspired look.

The Nail

If I struggled all day in traffic, it was for this. It was for this table with my wife and children who were really happy to see the big fish on the table. Life could be excellent if it weren't for those nails!

∞

The day was just beginning, and I was already driving toward my first destination. The advantage of my training as a tire repairman was that fixing a spare tire didn't take me any longer than drinking my morning coffee. The little repair shop was already open. I thanked Oliver, the small guy who was working on a wheel, by giving him a shove. I handed him my new tire with its machine screw and was satisfied to see him pull out the wretched little piece of metal. He carefully caulked the hole.

One of my cabs, which was being driven by François, should have arrived by now, as it needed repair. We figured François had overslept, and I prepared to dress him down. In the meantime, I decided to phone a friend to confirm that he would let me take out a loan in his name in order to buy a sixth car. I had already taken out loans in my name, in my wife's name, and in the names of some friends in order to pay for my small fleet. This worked well. With my cabs and repair shop, I earned enough for the monthly payments, and more money always came in. But the phone rang before I could dial out.

It was François calling. His cab and three other ones had been seized. He told me that the police were also going to come and seize mine. I didn't understand. I had done nothing illegal. But François vaguely explained to me that it was because of a rumor that was going around. People couldn't believe that a simple tire repairman like me could possess a fleet of five taxis. They were saying that I was lending my name to the city's mayor, who was earning money like this by illicitly employing a secret taxi company, and that I was his accomplice.

I was used to this kind of complication, and I dashed off to the prefecture. But things didn't look good. The commissioner, a European man, confirmed that he shared the suspicions that were being directed against me. I protested. I had the proper papers! He responded by treating me as a foreigner. It's true that I'm from Benin and immigrated to the Republic of Côte d'Ivoire, but the commissioner's response was rather ironic, coming from a white man. It was useless for me to explain that I had bills to pay and that I was going to justify the purchase of each one of my taxis. There was nothing that could be done. He insisted on immobilizing my cars!

I was stunned as I left the prefecture. Luckily, I knew a magistrate named Antoine. I often drove him in my cabs. He's an honest judge and a pastor who is from Benin like me. He understood the extent of my problem and went out of his way for me.

Time slowed down for two weeks, despite the coffee I was swallowing throughout the day. I became embedded in the tire repair shop. I think my employees had enough of having me underfoot and doing their work for them. Then I received the longed-for phone call. Antoine managed to get my cabs out of the hands of the police. That was good, but the immobilization of the vehicles for two weeks had cost me a lot of money. It was a catastrophe for my little company, which was always walking a tightrope!

I frenetically went back to work and put on my best-looking suits in order to give the impression that everything was going well. But there was no more St. Pierre fish in the house, and I looked at my family somberly. I was evasive and preoccupied with work and with the money I'd need to bring in. Despite my efforts, I had to call a creditor to ask him to wait. This had never happened to me.

Just a few days after my cabs started running again, one of them had an accident. Nobody was wounded, but the vehicle had to stay in the garage. I didn't need that. Then, a few days later, there was another accident that was even more serious. Here again, we were lucky: there were no serious injuries. But the car was good only for the junkyard. Needless to say, because I had had so much bad luck, all my friends and family members were convinced that I was bewitched. Someone had cast a spell on me. They had no doubt about that!

Benin is considered to be voodoo's birthplace. Everyone where I live, including priests, believes in the power of witches. But I've been headstrong since I was young. I have no respect for the power of healers or witches. I never wear any charms.

Yet, since my family insisted, and also, I guess, because I was a little distraught in the face of the succession of catastrophes that were descending upon me, I agreed to have a marabout deal with my cabs. He performed a little ceremony, which I thought was absurd, but I attended it anyway. When it was over, he equipped my cabs with charms. These were necklaces that were supposed to protect the cabs from bad spells. One of them, hanging from the rearview mirror, swayed as I drove, and I had the impression it was making fun of me.

At the end of the day, I went to the tire repair station, as I always did. Olivier approached me. He looked really distraught. Something serious had happened. He gave me the phone. I heard François crying at the end of the line. He explained that there had been an accident. "I ran over a child," he lamented. He had had a terrible accident—one more—but this time, a kid who was on the edge of the road died.

I went home and could articulate only "My cab killed a child." Léontine was stunned. She saw that I was desperate and simply needed to be alone. My head ached. I didn't see any way out. I desperately looked for a way to stop this pain that wasn't letting go of me. All that I was doing—all my works and efforts—resulted only in failures and catastrophes. They were worse than catastrophes. I ran to the bathroom, took a handful of pills, and got ready to swallow them with a glass of water. Right when I was going to shove the mixture in my mouth, I heard this in my head: "The life that was given to you isn't for you." My arm fell. I didn't have the right to end it like this. I was a Christian. God gave me life. I couldn't dispose of it. I finally fell asleep feeling sad but calmed down. The door to suicide was closed once and for all.

The next day, I got back in the car as if nothing had happened. I removed the charm that was still swaying from the rearview mirror and threw it out the window. I passed my tire repair shop and continued on the road. I finally left the city in which I had thought I had carved out a place for myself as a great entrepreneur. Soon the road was bad; it was unpaved. There were only trees that were punctuated with small houses of raw earth that had straw roofs. I took an even smaller lane and parked in the middle of nowhere.

I continued on foot, with only my Bible.

The big rock that I had noticed during a walk years before was right there. I sat down in its shade, with nothing around me but the African nature, some big trees, and the sounds of the forest. I read the Bible and prayed from morning until evening, without eating or drinking.

I recalled my childhood. I was a Christian—even a fervent one. I had never really stopped being one, but my faith had taken a back seat. How long had it been since I had participated in a Mass? How long had it been since I had prayed? I lost count. My frenetic activity and success had progressively taken me away from God. I had just discovered a very important truth—a fearsome trap. We don't suddenly lose faith. We let it break down piece by piece. It stops being at the heart of our lives and then drifts away without any apparent pain.

The Nail

I rediscovered the words of Tobit, the father of Tobias. They resonated in me. Tobias, who was blind and overwhelmed by misfortune, spoke to God: "And now deal with me according to thy pleasure; command my spirit to be taken up, that I may depart and become dust. For it is better for me to die than to live, because I have heard false reproaches, and great is the sorrow within me. Command that I now be released from my distress to go to the eternal abode; do not turn thy face away from me" (Tob. 3:6).

On the following days, I returned to the rock. It provided me with shade and had a symbolic strength for me. I was aware that up until then, I had built my life upon sand. Wealth and success can collapse from one day to the next, like sand. Faith is a rock. It doesn't matter what happens; it stands strong and within reach of those who are shipwrecked, as I was.

While thinking about this, I realized that I had gotten lost a long time ago. The terrible trials that I was going through were merely the revelation of a fall that went back to long before the horrible accident that was obsessing me.

DJOUGOU

It looked as if the asphalt was going to melt again. For how long had we been in a dry season? Probably for years! The atmosphere's stillness was disturbed only by the mirages that the heat emanated from the overheated ground. I was lying down at the edge of the steaming road. I was so dirty that I blended into the background. I was black with dirt, sticky, and hot—like the tar that people got me mixed up with. I could no longer tolerate my torn clothes, which were falling apart. But what clothes? I realized I no longer had a T-shirt. I had only a worn pair of frayed shorts. I looked around me. I had fallen asleep in the sunlight.

A few yards away, outside a shop, a mother had set up a table on which she had placed some fruits to sell. Her children were sleeping in the shade under the table. I would have liked to join them, but I knew they wouldn't want me to. I was scary. People said that I was bewitched, sick, and dangerous. To make matters worse, my right ear was missing. It had been ripped off in a fight.

I sensed the lady had given me a dirty look to tell me not to approach her children. I suspected that the shop's manager, who was in the back, was watching the scene and getting ready to intervene if I spoke to the lady. I felt sorry to be there in that outfit. I approached the lady to explain it to her.

But as I moved toward her, a sound like a siren practically tore my eardrums. I looked for its origin and realized that the lady was screaming. I tried to stop her: "No, no, don't scream. Don't be afraid. Everything is fine." But she continued.

I got hit in the shoulder, and blood flowed from the wound. Incredulously, I looked on the ground at the big stone, stained with red, that had just rolled by my foot. I was hurt and screamed in turn. But other stones were flying. They were coming from everywhere. I was being stoned!

I fled along the road. I ran, and everywhere people were looking at me. I felt that they all wanted to throw stones at me. I wanted to hide in the bush, but I lost my bearings. Only the main road was here. I was hurting and had had enough of the heat that made the remnants of my shorts stick to my legs. I took the shorts off and threw them over my shoulder. I had to get out of there! I had had enough of the sticky smoke and of this place where there was no shade or water for me. I wanted to see what was on the other side of the road. It was very congested at this time, but I had to try to cross it.

2

THE LOST ROCK

How had I gotten there? I was under my rock and overwhelmed with grief. The twenty-five-year-old businessman had let go of his tricks. My suit, which I now thought was ridiculous, stayed in the car. The Bible and I were all that was left, along with my memories.

As a child, I already liked work and success. But in recalling this time, it seemed to me that I knew how to keep things separate. If such a terrible tragedy had struck me then, I would never, for all that, have envisioned suicide. I would, of course, have been hurting, but such a gruesome thought as suicide would never have crossed my mind.

Now, I had been rescued by this strange voice that reminded me that my life didn't belong to me. I shuddered at the thought of what I had been preparing to do. I was going to add one tragedy to another one! I was going to leave my family in a terrible situation—the wife of a suicide victim and the sons of a suicide victim. Suicide is considered a curse in Africa.

This voice was Christ's. I didn't doubt it for a moment. Now that I saw the vanity of my life without Him, I would never again let Him go. I felt really bad for having let Him go for the world's illusions!

THEY ARE LIVING IN CHAINS

I saw myself again as a child who was diligent about attending Mass. That had stopped being important for me. Yet I saw that I hadn't become a bad man. My business was legal. I was taking care of my family. But I had lost sight of what was essential, and I tried to recall what I was missing.

I saw myself again in my native country, present-day Benin, which isn't very far from Avrankou, in the province of Porto-Novo. It seems that, at the time, what I'm talking about happened in the "Kingdom of Dahomey." It became independent in 1960, when I was eight years old. But this kind of change didn't reach my village—a group of homes that extended around a path. There was only a forest around it and no electricity or running water. We bathed in the backwater, where we drew water to drink and for washing dishes and laundry. For all that, I don't recall having been sick, except for having malaria, naturally, like everyone! At that time, the hospital was far away, and we went there only for extreme cases and when we had the resources to do it.

I remember, on the other hand, the miles that I walked to receive Communion. There were no priests here. This didn't prevent me from being interested in the Church. I was baptized on March 12, 1952. I participated in the choir, and I bought a Bible with one of my first paychecks, which was earned in Papa's field. It was this same dog-eared Bible that I was now pressing on my knees.

Mama, nevertheless, was an animist. She didn't wear any charms, but she shared the belief, which is common in Africa, in a hidden, mysterious God. Animism is broad. You shouldn't see only the quackery of pseudo witches in it. Mama didn't impose anything on me. She was satisfied with giving me herbal teas in order "for me to be in good health"; these were supposedly beneficial and used by sorcerers. I always refused to drink them, and she told me I was really stubborn!

My father was a sincere Christian, although he was polygamous. Luckily, the relationships have been good. I love my aunt and my half brothers and half sisters. This whole little tribe lives in harmony. I'm my mother's only son. I have been her everything!

I already see at this time a kid who liked to succeed. My father entrusted me with work in his cornfields. I even had to manage the mill that transformed the ears of corn into cornmeal. One day, my father gave me a dressing down: "The mill isn't yielding enough! You must work fast and make everyone pay!" I looked down. I was furious and was determined to earn a lot that day.

The villagers waited in line with their ears of corn. We had a small mill that was connected to a gasoline engine. The grinding cost six francs CFA (currency of French Africa). Then the people left with their cornmeal.

Once, a haughty older lady cut in front of the whole line and stood in front of me with her bag of corn. The others let her do it. She was a dreaded witch! I passed her corn on to the mill, gave her her bag of cornmeal, and said: "That will be six francs." She looked at me and scornfully threw three one-franc coins at me while replying: "I don't have six francs!" I kept standing. The lady towered over me, but I stuck to my guns: "You have to pay the price! I'm keeping the cornmeal until you bring me the three missing francs!"

At that moment, her silence weighed a ton. It was broken only by the small mill that was sputtering and turning behind me. The tall lady, wrapped in her boubou (an African garment), stared at the shrimp in his shorts. He staunchly faced her. The incredulous villagers gaped at the scene. The woman put her hand in her pocket. People shuddered, as if she were going to pull out a gun. She took out the remaining money and handed it to me. I took it in exchange for her bag of cornmeal. She left determined to cast a spell on the entire village.

I continued to work as if nothing had happened, but people looked serious. They looked at me sadly and were persuaded that that was the last time they would see me. Mama learned about this and was naturally devastated. Yet I made it through the night, contrary to the predictions! The next day, everyone was persuaded that I myself was a sorcerer! I didn't suspect anything.

How could the same adult man have accepted hanging a charm in his car? I had gotten lost at some point in my story. I remembered the child I was. He would have a hard time recognizing me.

∞

I prayed with my half sisters and half brothers every day. I also prayed by myself. I don't recall that this was imposed on me. It was like a natural breath in my day. The Gospel imperceptibly guided my actions.

I remember Soujonou. He was an elderly man whom I often visited when I was thirteen years old. When I went to see this man the first time, I was not thinking. I didn't tell myself that I had to disrupt his solitude in order to do "something good." I just talked to him. He responded to me naturally and enjoyed our conversation. He was small and rather shy with others but was, in fact, very jovial and humorous in his private life. Few people in the village knew his real face, for this man didn't have a family and, therefore, had no one to watch over him. Most of the time, families in Africa take good care of their elders, but those who are alone, like Soujonou, are abandoned. I was amazed to see the good that it did him to have me visit him in order simply to spend a little time together to talk and joke. This was also good for me.

I was known for being interested in isolated elderly people. Some of them knocked on my door to ask if I was home. My mother sometimes had to put them outside in order for me to do my homework. She didn't have to do a lot of coaxing. She saw that I was conscientious. I listened in school. I did my homework and my reading. I liked my classes and school. My teachers and friends appreciated me. Despite this, there was nothing to be done about my schoolwork. The information didn't go in. Writing and things on paper simply didn't get etched in my brain. I retained oral things very well. But as soon as they were written, you could no longer count on me! So I preferred to abandon my studies after fifth grade. My father let me do it. He did as much when he was my age. He said it wasn't very important because I was working well in the fields. I've often regretted this. I think that further studies would have helped me to talk and understand some things.

But at the time, I left the notebooks to the students in my village. The fields, the corn, and odd jobs took up all my time. I worked well on the whole. I liked concrete achievements that offered tangible results. I was not tempted by the games of friends who were my age, even if I happened to kick a soccer ball occasionally.

In addition to visiting older people, I really enjoyed driving my father's motorcycle. I sometimes fell, but this didn't stop me. When they heard the engine roar in the village, people said to themselves, "Here comes Grégoire" and prudently stayed far away from the road. Speed already fascinated me.

Once, at the end of Mass, I went out to warm up the engine, and I took advantage of this to engage in a race. But I had an accident, and the motorcycle was ruined. Unable to accept responsibility for my stupidity, I left for Cotonou, where I joined a friend of the family. He found me a job as a housekeeper, but the job soon wore me out. After three days of washing laundry and cleaning floors, I went back home, like the prodigal son. Not surprisingly, my father yelled at me, but my mother was very happy to see me again. She had been worried to death.

This impromptu and rather pitiful trip gave me a desire to make a fresh start. I felt like going further and trying my luck elsewhere. I thought more about it and decided to talk to Mama about it when I was sixteen. She, of course, refused and got all worked up. How could she agree to have her only son go away?

But I liked my idea. I wanted to leave my village and have a better future than I could expect there. I wanted to go to Côte d'Ivoire, for it seemed that I could earn a good living there. A lot of young people my age took this trip to the west, for the country offered economic opportunities. Lucien had left our village for that country ten years ago. When he came back, he was well dressed and driving a car. The young people looked at him with stars in their eyes!

My parents knew me. They knew I wouldn't give in. In the end, my father agreed, and soon it was time for the great departure. When one of the village's elderly men heard of my decision, he exclaimed: "Grégoire is leaving? Who will come see us now?" Yet, my desire for adventure was stronger than anything.

I see myself again folding my shirts and preparing my little bundle. I felt like conquering the world! I was carefully wrapping up the money that Papa had given me. He paid me something to travel with along with an envelope of money, which I hid in the bottom of my bag. I think he was proud of me without daring to show it. Mama strived not to look too devastated.

I went to the home of a friend named Michel in Bouaké in Côte d'Ivoire. He had to house me and give me a job as an apprentice tire repairer. The envelope was destined for him. It had to be used to pay for my laundry and food.

I was in the school of hard knocks in Michel's workshop. Big and strong, the man didn't spare his employees. I learned to get tires off trucks. It was a strenuous job! We didn't have the equipment that we have now. In order to get a broken tire off, you had to bang on it hard with a hammer. The simple fact of handling wheels was a problem for me at first. They were very heavy!

That's where I learned to patch and shave tires so they could be used again. The clients didn't want to change them. They wanted them repaired. So we had to make sure the tires held up. We salvaged them and got by. I worked well but didn't earn anything. I didn't get a salary as an apprentice. Sometimes, a client gave me a tip, but Michel even took that!

Unfortunately, Michel told me that the envelope I gave him was lost and that I had to write my father to ask him for more money. He told me: "You must write your father for him to pay me. I don't have enough to feed and house you anymore." That revolted me. I didn't want Papa to get scammed. I wrote my letter under Michel's attentive gaze. I started my text as Michel dictated it to me: "Dear Papa, I'm writing you on behalf of our friend Michel. There's a problem with the money envelope …" But Michel didn't know how to read — or barely — and I slipped a message in the middle of my text to my father's attention: "Never send a franc to Michel. I handed the envelope to him, and I'm sure he still has it. He's trying to swindle you, and I couldn't bear that. I'm ready to suffer in his workshop, but I don't want him to squeeze out more than he's already taken."

The ploy succeeded, and I worked in the workshop more than ever. I made friends among the other mechanics. They saw that I worked hard. One day, one of them called me to tell me my father was on the phone.

My father told me on the phone that Mama was crying and that she wanted me to come home. I didn't even have enough to pay for the trip! But, at any rate, there was no question about it. I wasn't going to come back home without any money. So I told my father that I was working and earning my living well. I also told him I was going to send a picture of myself to Mama. One of the employees lent me a suit, and I got my picture taken smiling, with a little note saying that I was earning my living and would return once I made my fortune.

I was far from it. I looked for a way to work on my own rather than enrich "our friend" Michel. I spoke to my colleagues about it, and, in the end, I found a solution. Two friends lent me a little money for the equipment I needed to start my own tire repair company.

I bought a little toolbox and some patches. The basic equipment was meager, but I could not afford a tire inflator. I had my own idea for that. I made the rounds of the gas stations and offered to set up my business at one of them. The deal was simple. I set up my business there, and I got to use the station's tire inflator for free. And my presence would bring more customers for the gas station. Those who stopped in to have a tire fixed would probably take advantage of the opportunity to gas up, which would work out well for the boss.

My deal suited Karim, a Muslim man who was about fifty years old. He really welcomed me, and I set up my little workbench near his station's tire inflator. In the beginning, I had only a table that I made and scrubbed and on which I arranged my basic equipment. I watched out for the clients and talked to those who filled their tanks. I introduced myself: "Hello, I'm new here, and I fix tires." I was well received. People liked to talk while we filled up their vehicles' tanks.

The first jobs quickly arrived. I installed my patches and reinflated the tires. The hardest thing was to take care of the trucks. Their wheels were very hard to get off. I didn't have a hammer, so I struck them with a big stone. That also worked, but with that method, you have to pay more attention to your fingers. The clients saw that I wasn't just hanging around. They found that their tires were quickly repaired. So I soon had work for practically the whole day. At the end of the first month, I paid back the money that I had borrowed for the tools. I felt triumphant!

Despite the heat, the smell of tires burned by friction, and the African sun, I was enthusiastic. Money was coming in, and I bought myself some nice equipment.

It seems to me that that's where "it" started.

∝∞

I now realized that in the shade of my rock. While I was applying all of my energy to building my business, with the obsession of returning to my country with a suit and a beautiful car, I stopped reading the Gospel. I no longer prayed or went to Mass. God was no longer the center of my concerns. The exhilaration of the company and of success occupied me to the point at which I forgot what was most important. Everyone must be warned about this: most often, we don't suddenly lose the faith. It's imperceptibly eroded. We gradually renounce it without knowing it—and then we wake up totally lost!

Yet I held on to my identity as a Christian. I was aware of this while thinking about Douha.

Douha was sixteen years old. She was the station owner's daughter, and she had beautiful black eyes. She also liked me. I went out with her a little, but I didn't try to flirt. I wanted to get married, and she did too. I went to talk with her parents, who kindly received me.

Karim took his wife, Douha's mother, and his daughter as witnesses and said, while smiling: "I can't wish for a better boy than Grégoire for my daughter. He's serious, and he works, but he has to become a Muslim in order for me to give him my daughter." He even planned to buy us a house and wanted to give me responsibilities at his station. I appreciated this man, who I knew was honest, but I couldn't do what he was asking of me. I was a Christian and would keep being one. I didn't really practice anymore, but I would never have thought about doubting my faith.

We left as good friends, and I hoped that Karim would change his mind, but for the following days, the situation remained at a standstill. I'd later learn that Douha was forced into marriage with a man her family had chosen for her.

On the other hand, things continued to go well in the store. The incident didn't change my relationship with the station's manager. I got more and more work. A man who left his native country, as I did two years before, came knocking on my door. This providential guy was called Marc, and I hired him right away. I was a boss and was hardly twenty years old!

DJOUGOU

I don't know how, but I returned to the sticks. I recall a car
that plowed toward me and avoided me at the last moment.
Then there was nothing more. I had a stomachache. I hoped
I wasn't wounded.

I was better off in the sticks than in the city. There
was shade there, and there weren't those cars that make
that noise that bores into my head! But hunger twisted my
stomach. I had lived here for a long time—in the sticks and
the city. How did I feed myself in the past? Not too well if I
believed my protruding ribs. Yet I was really sure there was
food to eat in town. Thus, I went back to the noise and the
heat without shade.

3

CUSTOMARY WEDDING

So who was this little businessman who was starting his company by working hard? It was, of course, the same hardworking and serious kid whom his friends appreciated in school—even if he wasn't very successful. This time I *was* successful! I had just hired a guy who, like me, arrived from his hometown with only the clothes on his back.

I saw Marc gratefully working for my company. I wasn't gentle with him. I pushed him so that he could give the best of himself. But I quickly saw that he worked well, and I was proud of him! I had just closed the loop in a way. I had gotten out of Michel's clutches and was, in turn, assigning work.

∞

In early 1976, I went to downtown Bouaké, with its gleaming store windows set up in a European style. The mannequins displayed their Colgate smiles on their artificially whitened skin. (In order to be considered beautiful, you couldn't have skin that was too dark.) They fit into well-tailored suits with ease. The women wore pristine, tight-fitting outfits.

I went in and bought myself my first suit. I got one that was simple and elegant—in a word, serious. It was the outfit of a man who had succeeded. This time, I didn't borrow it for a picture. It was mine for good. I placed it—carefully folded—on the seat of my car. For, yes, I now had my own car. It was not well made, but it was mine!

Thus equipped, I returned to the village to visit my family. I drove with an exhilarating feeling of freedom while thinking again about the way I had made it work—full of hope—with just my money envelope in my pocket. I went through Ghana and Togo and returned to my native land.

My family, of course, celebrated my return to the village. They rushed to greet me and eagerly listened to the story of my success in Benin. Mama was ecstatic. She experienced each of my saga's episodes. She shuddered when I told her about the way I had to remove the truck tires with a big stone. She clapped when I reached my conclusion and related how I had hired Marc in my company. She was so proud of me!

I left to greet my neighbors and found the door shut in front of Sojounou's home. The poor elderly man had died! I then realized that in my new life, I never had the time to visit the elderly people who needed it so much. But I had a lot of other things to do, and I left this thought aside.

I asked to speak to my parents on the evening of this festive day. All three of us sat in the living room. We looked serious. I started to explain: "My dear parents, I'm now earning my living. I'm a successful man. I don't want to live a chaotic life. So I wish to get married."

There was silence. They looked at me, and I could see in their eyes that they were joyful.

My mother responded: "Your sisters and I will take care of everything, Grégoire. We are so pleased!" She glowed, smiled at me, and disappeared into the nearby room, from which I heard giggles and playful chattering. My sisters, of course, had guessed everything, and they couldn't have hoped for more than to take care of my wedding. It would be a customary Benin wedding; that was, above all, women's business. I assume it's like this everywhere.

As soon as my announcement was made, the house was buzzing with feminine activity. My sisters were talking and laughing a lot and started to examine my possible candidates. The next day, they "discreetly" visited families in which the rare gem could be found. The news of my intention to marry crossed the region more efficiently than if it had been announced in the evening newspaper. My sisters didn't delay in finding the perfect wife for me, and they described her to me: "Lovely and serious. She comes from a Christian family and is eighteen years old." I relied on their judgment.

They made an appointment, and I went to the young lady's home in a procession with my parents and sisters. We were a bit tense, for the stakes were important. A customary wedding is serious. If it is broken, there are terrible consequences for the relationships of both families! But we were very well received. I saw Léontine between her two parents. She was a delightful young lady who timidly smiled. We didn't speak to each other while the parents and sisters greeted each other. The room was soon animated. Everyone was talking at the same time. The parents immediately got along with each other. The atmosphere was friendly. Léontine and I were the only ones who didn't participate in this exuberant atmosphere.

This was a decisive time in my life. I was experiencing a lot of inner peace. I wasn't at all doubtful. I prayed and gave thanks: "She's the one that God wanted for me. May He be blessed." The conversations subsided, and Mama asked me: "Do you agree to do this? Do you want Léontine to become your wife?"

THEY ARE LIVING IN CHAINS

I got up, looked Léontine in the eyes, and loudly and intelligibly said, so that everyone could be a witness: "I want you to be my spouse. You're beautiful, and I love you." Everyone clapped. Then Léontine responded in turn: "I also want you to be my spouse." From this moment on, the atmosphere was festive, for the families were honored to be united by this kind of "engagement," even if there was nothing official and no wedding yet.

During the conversation, we discovered that there was an apparently insurmountable difficulty. Léontine's parents didn't want their daughter to leave for Côte d'Ivoire. I couldn't abandon the company that I had just started. What would we live on here in Benin? We all stuck to our guns and went back home a little annoyed. Mama would have liked to have me stay for Léontine's sake, but I didn't want to make her live in Benin, where our future children would be in poverty. There wasn't enough work for everyone.

Then my sisters went hunting again and didn't take long to find me a potential new companion. But I refused to go see her. I replied to my sisters: "Léontine was your first choice, and I defer to your judgment. She's really the right wife for me." For several days, somber looks and anxious conversations replaced the laughter.

Then my sisters came back smiling. In the face of my inflexibility, Léontine's parents agreed to have her join me in Côte d'Ivoire! I was full of joy and thanked Heaven again! From then on, there was no longer any question about this union in the families and even, to a greater extent, in the village. The two future spouses met, and then love triumphed over the reluctance of the future wife's parents. That made for a good story that fueled people's conversations. Yet the marriage preparation wasn't very important. It wasn't a matter of a big feast, as in Christian or Muslim weddings. The customary wedding occurs in the intimacy of families. I imagine this is a strange thing to a Westerner. The groom isn't invited to this sort of wedding; it is, above all, for families.

People were busy gathering the "dowry" that was to be provided, for the man's family is the one that makes the gifts. There's a specific list of things to give for the home: clothes, wrap skirts, dishes, and so forth. Therefore, my parents and sisters returned to bring their gifts to Léontine, and the matter was settled.

I suppose that this way of getting married will stun my European readers, but things are also changing in Benin. Now young people are doing the "finding" themselves. They are no longer calling on their families. For all that, I don't sense that the results are better. There are so many separations and infidelities. In any case, for Léontine and me, ours was a good union. We weren't united in the Church at that time. We did that afterward. I'll talk about it later. But, thanks to our families, we were united. I've never regretted my sisters' choice. Léontine is a marvelous wife, who has faithfully supported me in my most difficult decisions, even when everyone tried to discourage us. She gave me six children, and each one of them is a source of great pride for us!

∞

We settled down in Côte d'Ivoire, where I found us a good house. I gave myself entirely to my tire repair company. I was in the thick of it—managing accounts and personnel and changing tires. I thought about shopping for a cab. The idea came to me while talking with cab drivers, who were my faithful clients because of the wear and tear on their vehicles. I now had in mind the amount we could hope to gain in a month. I never rested on my laurels. Seeing that everything was going well, I bought a new car and hired a driver. In a short time, my cab brought in more money than my investment in it.

I had business in my blood without having gone to school. I didn't hoard money and never stayed still! Each coin was reinvested to enlarge the company.

The children arrived—first Bruno, then Moïse-Florent. I was a happy man. Everything was going so well!

∞

Somewhere in Bouaké, one of the cabs that I was so proud of killed an innocent child. Nothing can explain or justify such a horrible accident. Because of this tragedy, I had been about to add another one by killing myself! What a terrible shame. I saw the sun go down while I was under my rock. I left it and was still full of grief. But at least I knew who I was. The idea of suicide was dismissed for good, and I'll never go back there again.

It would soon be dark. Night falls quickly in this region. So I went on my way. While I was driving, I told myself that I'd had lost a day of work—that if I had returned to the workshop, I could have more quickly moved it forward, or I could have gone to see this creditor to try to delay a payment. I rejected these ideas that were bombarding me. It was in this frenetic activity that I got lost in the past. I no longer wanted to get lost. I wanted to find my faith again. The rest would come as well. Jesus Himself assures us of this!

LÉONIE

"I beg you," I told them, "not to do this." But nothing could be done about it. And I saw the scene from the outside—as if I had gone outside my body. I felt a little sorry for the poor young girl who was crying and who was saying that she would behave well, but I let it slide. Together, they decided that the hospital would be of no use. The marabout couldn't do anything to help. So she had to be put out of harm's way in order for her not to provoke a catastrophe. They said she was a witch and that she had a bad spirit.

I came back to myself behind my parents' house. I had a big cord around my neck, whose other end was attached to the prickly acacia where I played as a child. They tied me up like a goat to a stake. The cord was squeezing my neck. I was afraid it was going to strangle me. When I got restless, I felt my pulse in the cord and sensed I was going to explode! I was enraged. I tried to bite it, but it didn't do any good. They had left, and they wouldn't have listened anyway. So I sat on the ground and tried to calm myself and get my head straight. Sometimes, I heard snatches of phrases. They were talking about wood and chains. They were going to shackle me so that I couldn't escape. How much longer? When would they see that I wasn't a danger to anyone?

The night fell. They left me there. The more I thought about it, the more my conviction grew. They would never let me go. I was sixteen years old, and I was dead to them. They could just as well have buried me alive. I was afraid they would find something stronger than the big cord to tie me with. It was hard, but I had good teeth. So I patiently gnawed it off, strand by strand. I was losing pieces of teeth, but the fear of ending my days shackled was stronger than anything. Strands of rope gave way and stuck between my teeth.

A little later, I was completely alone, and I didn't know where I was going. It was dark. I hardly saw anything on the little path that crossed the forest, and the branches were whipping me as I ran. Yet I didn't dare slow down for fear that I'd be recaptured. I'd never accept being locked up again. I was alone and afraid. But I preferred that to reliving my confinement.

As I came to this conclusion, I made out a moving shape on the edge of the path. It was surely an animal. I approached it and saw a round, pale little face that was looking at me from the thickets that surrounded the bushes. While I stared at it, it disappeared. I continued on my way, despite everything. Then, I heard some strange voices. They told me never to return, and this was what I intended to do.

4

SIFTING OUT

When I returned home, the whole household was sleeping. Léontine had left my dinner on the table and had carefully arranged
the utensils. A cover kept the plate warm. The children were peacefully sleeping, far removed from my financial problems. Léontine
worked in the market during the day. She was the one who now
brought back food for the household. I felt wounded in my pride
as a "serious" working man, as my parents had called me.

But perhaps it was essentially a good thing. I now saw the
place that success held in my life. My "treasure"—what I valued
most—must not be success. I sensed that I had ventured far from
what was really important. I ate a little rice while repeating the
events in my head over and over again. I didn't touch the chicken
that my wife had thoughtfully cooked for me. I decided to fast. As
of today, I would fast for forty days, contenting myself with eating
only what was necessary each night. After finishing my meal, I
prayed in the dark. I went through all the emotions—rage against
my stupidity, the sorrow of seeing that I was making my family
carry my burden, and despair when I thought of this poor kid who
had been killed. I put everything at the feet of Jesus. I went to bed
and was more exhausted than if I had worked all day.

I tried to look good the next morning. I didn't swallow even a glass of water, but I got ready for my workday and joked with Léontine and the children. I felt empty inside. My gestures were those of an automaton. When I drove to the station, I felt that I wasn't the one driving the car. I arrived at the workshop, where I was greeted respectfully. But I had a sense of unreality, as if my employees were speaking to someone other than me. Whom did this mechanic, who was wiping his hand on his pants before shaking my hand, think he was dealing with? With the boss? I wasn't a big deal anymore.

There wasn't a lot of work that day. This was unlucky for me, as I was wishing for activity. On the other hand, I was told that one of the creditors had called me.

I took the phone and put my best foot forward. I got a lump in my stomach when I heard the dial tone. I was hoping that the person I was going to speak to wasn't there and that I could simply leave a message with his secretary.

"Hello?"

"Yes, it's Grégoire. It seems that you tried calling me?"

"Yes, and you know very well why. You were supposed to give me my money back yesterday. I'm still waiting!"

"I beg you, be patient with me. We're working as much as we can in the workshop. I'm going to send you what I can right away. The rest will arrive later with interest."

"I'm tired of waiting! You're always making me hang around waiting because of your monkey business!"

"You must not believe what people tell you. I'm not messing around! I've always done honest work. Listen, I will drop the money off in person at the end of the day."

The man I was speaking to angrily hung up. I put the phone down and felt Marc gazing at me. He obviously understood the situation. Perhaps he was already looking for another position elsewhere? I took what was left in the cash box. It would cover only a fourth of my debt. But perhaps it would be enough to show my goodwill.

Meanwhile it was time to get to work! I was determined to earn all the remaining money I owed. But as it happened, there was no work that day. I started changing the wheel of an old pickup truck, but I was aware that Marc was just standing there. A week earlier, in this situation, I would have been on the road with one of my cabs, but I had put them all up for sale. I didn't want to hear any more talk about cabs! I gave the hammer to Marc and got back into my car. I was going to go back under my rock.

In the peace of the forest, I was hoping to find some of the carefree, optimistic child I had been. I had to convince myself that my financial worries were not so important and that God would provide. I read, in particular, in the Gospel of St. Matthew: "Look at the birds in the sky; they do not sow or reap, they gather nothing into barns, yet your heavenly Father feeds them. Are you not more important than they?" (6:26).

"God will provide." I pressed the Bible against my forehead so that these words would enter my skull and free me of the anxiety that had been twisting my gut for a week. Sometimes nothing could be done. I was afraid of being completely alone under this big rock—just a lunatic who was wasting his time rather than struggling to get out of his financial worries. Up until then, I had been on fire. I saw difficulties as mountains to climb, and that had worked out well. But now I had to let go and stop wanting to control everything. I hadn't known anxiety and doubt, but now they were fully present. What should I do? Why wasn't I finding a solution? Finally, I prayed. I had never understood before that the mere fact of laying your burden at God's feet was in itself a prayer. It is, however, a very common attitude among the people in the Bible. Didn't the psalmist call out: "Out of the depths I call to you, LORD!" (Ps. 130:1)? I lived like this—fasting, praying, and worrying—without experiencing joy.

∞

"Praise and glory to Your name. Alleluia! Alleluia!" Léontine and I sang from the heart in the midst of the faithful. Bruno, who was at my feet, also sang, and Moïse-Florent clapped his hands. We were in the middle of a joyous crowd of parishioners. It wasn't hard to find a Mass every Sunday in Bouaké. I appreciated this opportunity that I had taken so little advantage of before. I was happy and had found my niche with the parishioners here. It was a priceless respite in these weeks of uncertainty.

The priest who celebrated Mass was a white man named Fr. Pasquier. He came from France and was an authentic missionary who had devoted his life to carrying the Gospel to places far from his native land.

∞

My financial problems didn't get better. I was like a boxer on the ropes who was taking one hit after another. Creditors distrusted me. They knew I couldn't meet my deadlines. But I had friends. People saw that I still worked and ended up paying my debts. So I survived, week after week.

Léontine was a daily support during these days of doubt and anxiety. She never blamed me. Even in the most difficult moments, thanks to her, our house breathed peace. Yet I must not have always been good company. I often traveled far and wide. However, I insisted that our children attend school regularly. I now saw how important this was.

One night, when I was sitting on the bed, in the grip of my reflections, Léontine sat next to me and said, "Grégoire, I'm pregnant." I was really perplexed by this news, which should have filled me with joy. How were we going to get by? We weren't earning a lot of money. My debtors were still after me, and I was going to have another mouth to feed. I tried not to look disturbed, but Léontine sensed it. She didn't say anything and smiled. How I envied her confidence at that moment!

I went back to my daily life: my prayers, work, and endless debates with creditors. But, in the clear blue sky, everything had changed.

I can't talk here about a precise day or a particular moment. These problems that had so vehemently monopolized me had subtly taken a back seat. They were still very present. It was my duty to take them in hand, but they stopped hiding what was essential from me. I can't say precisely when this occurred. But what I had asked for in the past—that I could put Jesus back into the center of my life—was granted to me. God didn't come like thunder or an earthquake. He swept over me discreetly, but completely—like a breeze.

Nothing had changed on the outside. I was still working night and day. I worked relentlessly and got very few results as a reward. Yet something happened that changed everything. My wish had been granted! I'm still grateful to the Lord when I think about this priceless gift that was given to me.

It was also at this time that I befriended Fr. Pasquier. I was intrigued by this priest who had left his diocese in Angers. I had seen how close he was to the poorest people. Thus, I went to him for Confession, and he replied: "Don't worry; your problem is now my problem." He knew about my very precarious financial situation, and yet one day in 1981 he invited me go on a pilgrimage with him to the Holy Land. I, of course, replied that I didn't have the money for that, but he assured me that everything would be paid for. He thought this would be a trip that would bear much fruit, and he managed to find the funds. I was very grateful to this priest for his offer, which I accepted. I was going to see the land where Jesus lived!

Shortly after I departed on the pilgrimage, Joseph, one of my most virulent creditors, learned that I had left by plane. He went to see my magistrate friend Antoine, who laughed and told me about the scene later. After Joseph discovered that I was on a pilgrimage, he seethed with rage. He was persuaded that I was making fun of him. He said: "He has money to take a plane but not to reimburse me! He'll see when he returns—I'm going to give him a hard time!"

I didn't have to wait until then. I was already going through a hard time.

∞

On the pilgrimage, while I was gazing out the bus window, I kept mumbling, "No. It's not possible." But what fascinated me about what I saw wasn't at all spiritual. This trip was my first connection with the Western world. I saw the clean lines of the airport and the buildings. The wide, paved road awakened my dreams of speed! The West is a culture shock that is hard to imagine for an African person. This explains why despite all its failures, so many of us still see the West as an Eldorado.

When we reached Jerusalem, we left the bus behind and entered the sacred city humbly on foot—a little like a Muslim who takes his shoes off before entering a mosque.

We were housed not far from the Holy Sepulcher. I walked there with beating heart in the wee hours when it was dark. I was moved like a child by the idea that I was placing my footsteps in those of Jesus. The first One I call on in the morning when I wake up and the last One I think of at night had lived here! Jesus suffered His Passion where this strange church—as dark as a cave and as exuberant as an orthodox cathedral—was standing. A colorful crowd rushed in. These were people from everywhere—people of all colors who spoke languages I didn't understand. I reviewed St. John's description of the elect in the book of Revelation: "After this I had a vision of a great multitude, which no one could count, from every nation, race, people, and tongue. They stood before the throne and before the Lamb" (7:9).

Later in the day, we got on the bus again and headed north by crossing the desert's slopes. This was a fascinating vision for a young man who had known only the tropical climate of his native Africa. I recalled the scenes in the Gospel that took place on these slopes—scenes I had heard about since my early youth. I imagined Jesus, the apostles, and the people coming to hear His voice.

Then we went up north again to the green area around Lake Tiberias. We crossed the lake by boat. I was a bit ashamed to ride a big motorboat, whereas Jesus and His disciples were content with simple wooden boats. But when we reached the middle of the lake, a storm suddenly broke out, and the big boat at once seemed tiny in the face of the elements. I can testify that the storms on Lake Tiberias aren't a myth. Everyone hangs on! A lot of us weren't used to the sea and started to panic. The water poured into the boat, which was laboriously turned around toward the shore.

I must interrupt the story here to explain that at least three times in my life, I did some rather crazy things without any sense of danger. I experienced the first of these three moments on this boat.

I danced on the boat while my compatriots panicked. I didn't particularly have my sea legs and was laughing and singing: "Glory to God! We're experiencing the Gospel!" Again, I saw the disciples who were frightened by the storm. But be assured, I didn't think I was Jesus. I was simply happy and filled with a childlike joy to see the texts that I had been reading for so long take shape for our group of pilgrims. I welcomed this moving experience as a true gift from Heaven.

The boat finally berthed where, according to tradition, the risen Jesus ate the fish on the beach with His disciples. The storm calmed down almost as soon as in the episode reported by St. Mark (4:35-41), and we dried up quickly in Palestine's sun.

We sat in a circle around Fr. Pasquier, and he commented on some of the episodes of the Gospel that took place around the lake. He concluded by saying: "Each Christian provides a rock to build up the Church. I'd like you to ask yourselves: What rock do I bring to build up the Church?" This question was turning around in my head. In fact, this question will never leave me. I'm aware that the Church isn't simply the concern of priests and religious. I started to wonder: "What rock am I going to lay down for the Church?"

AMIDOU

I beg you, if someone receives this message, he must cut the chain that is binding my neck. I don't know why, but it's hurting me, as if it were burning. I said this to those who were coming to feed me at times, but they didn't hear me. They were like zombies. I was dead to them, and they were dead to me. I pulled on the chain at first, but this skinned me, and the metal didn't move. I was attached to a tree—a tree that was so big that I would have been hard-pressed to cut it with an ax, if I had one. Yet I was young and strong! There was no way out. My universe was reduced to my chain's two-meter length.

I considered all the possible ways of escape. I hoped that my jailers would take pity on me. But I was still there. Sometimes, I came to hope that someone could hear me through a form of telepathy. I screamed inside my head. It seems that there are people who can hear this kind of call.

I had been trying for a long time. It didn't work. I tirelessly went through my two-meter radius whose every detail and root I knew.

5

MY LITTLE PEBBLE

After returning from my pilgrimage, I took up my busy life again. But it imperceptibly became more and more joyous. Joseph, the angry creditor, didn't find me right away. Luckily, he seemed to have forgotten me. I looked for other jobs besides my work in my little garage. While I was talking with one of my brothers, he told me that running a print shop was a good way to earn a living. In the 1980s, a lot of institutions in Benin needed to print documents, and printers were still rare. My brother's idea interested me, but I didn't have the money to buy a printer.

A few days later, one of the parish's teachers fortuitously called me on the phone to talk to me about a problem:

"Grégoire, the printer in the high school is broken, and they are very annoyed. Could you come and have a look at it?"

"But you know, I repair cars, not printers."

"They don't have anyone, and you know a lot about mechanics. So if you could look at this, it would be very helpful to us."

"I will come and see, but I can't promise you anything."

So I went to play the troubleshooter with some tools that I borrowed from the garage. I was rather stunned by the coincidence between my conversation with my brother and this printer problem.

When I arrived at the high school, I discovered that there were not one but two printers. Neither one was working. I read the instructions and opened the hood. My garage tools were too big for this delicate machinery with plastic cogs. However, I started to understand how it worked.

There were some broken pieces to change and some rather delicate to manipulate, but nothing that a little time and money couldn't fix. So I went to see the school's principal and offered him this: "I'll repair these free of charge if you give me one of these two machines." The deal suited him very well. In fact, he had bought the second machine because the first one had stopped working. Within a few days, I went looking for the piece, tinkered a little, and with an investment of thirty thousand CFA francs,[1] I ended up being an owner of one of those renowned printers!

I didn't have any trouble finding work for it. Soon, it was purring like a big cat. Some storekeepers and restaurant owners ordered brochures from me, which came out of my machine at their regular fast pace. In my previous life, I would have envisioned bundles of money coming out of the machine as if by magic. But I had stopped looking at things in this way. The money was coming in, and that was very good. But I was no longer going to let myself be attracted by a profit motive or a company's euphoria.

Several days before the new deadline that Joseph had set, I went to see him with the money I owed him—including interest. He gloated and said: "This is another Grégoire who has come back from the Holy Land! This is a Grégoire who pays all his debts." It was true that my money problems were being resolved, but this wasn't enough to satisfy me. I looked elsewhere—for the "little pebble" that I wanted to bring humbly to build up the Church.

---

[1]   About fifty U.S. dollars today.

I didn't initially look for tangible social action. I started with the intention to set up a prayer group with some friends from the parish. We met each week, entrusted our intentions to one another, recited the Rosary, and read Scripture.

One evening, one of the members of the group entrusted us to pray for the sick child of one of his friends—a Muslim neighbor. The child had been discharged from the university hospital and was dying. We went to the child's home, and his mother accepted our presence, despite the religious difference. We all prayed together for the healing of this little boy, who hadn't been eating for several days.

The next day, the mother came to see us. She was amazed. She kissed each one of us and said: "Your God is very powerful! My boy started eating again this morning. He's doing better!" We were stunned and joyful. I gathered the members of the group together and said to them: "You've seen how powerful and effective prayer is! It healed and did some good. There are a lot of people who are alone and sick. Let's go see them and pray for them!"

A hubbub followed my announcement. Everyone agreed, but where would we start? Naturally, I went to the nearest hospital. It happened to be the St. Camillus Hospital. I had no idea who this great saint was, and yet it wasn't a coincidence that God put him in our path.

We visited the sick in the hospital and offered to pray for them. I don't recall that any of them refused this. Animists, Christians, and Muslims all wanted to benefit from the protection we provided with our prayers. We invited those who were mobile to join us in a room where we all prayed together. We quickly became friends with the nursing staff, who appreciated our support. We helped the patients feel better. Many were alone. The staff continually walked a fine line trying to discern how to help the patients.

I didn't know much about hospitals before this experience. No one in my family had suffered from any serious illness or accident. But our prayer group got to know some patients and discovered their living conditions. We saw that those who weren't regularly visited by their families didn't even have enough to eat.

The cafeteria wasn't free. The patients who could pay for only an operation received nothing more. After I saw this, I spoke to the prayer group at the end of one of our meetings: "We are praying for the sick and visiting them. That's very good, but is that enough? You see, as I do, that many patients don't even have enough to eat! We could, with a little effort, offer some simple meals for them to get their strength back. It's written in the Letter of James that just as the body without the soul is dead, likewise, faith without works is dead!" (2:26).

My intervention provoked some lively discussions in the group. Some agreed. Others thought we were going too far. But, in the end, the idea of a weekly festive meal was adopted. We pooled our efforts to make great dishes that we brought to the sick.

I bought a gigantic fish at the market. I bought the biggest pot in the hardware store. My two arms couldn't reach around it! Léontine put the pot over three burners and started to cook. The children gathered around it. They were fascinated by the pot, which they thought was a bathtub. The onion and pieces of chicken sizzled in the oil. We threw a mountain of canned tomatoes and the fish into the pot. Along with lots of rice, it made a nourishing dish for the patients. The wonderful aroma from the pot, still hot, filled my car. We were so happy to furnish this first feast! I never felt I was providing a service that cost me anything.

Like the Magi loaded with gifts, the members of the prayer group arrived at the hospital. The atmosphere, which was usually rather morose, became festive. This was really a lesson from God, who gives us missions that don't exceed our strength. We got a lot of joy in feeding the hospital patients with minimal effort. Afterward, I'd have more thankless missions, but this one was the first one to put me on the path I was now taking.

Encouraged by our success, we decided to create the St. Camillus Association on that date in 1981. I'm often introduced as the founder, but this is false. Jesus is the founder. I'm only His servant. I didn't know who St. Camillus was at the time, but when I read his biography, I realized that no patron saint could have been more fitting. St. Camillus de Lellis was a giant in the field of charity who started his life as a distracted youth before completely devoting himself to supporting the sick. He assures us that "the sick are the apple of God's eye and His heart, and those who serve the sick serve God Himself."

In 1982, Léontine and I were active parishioners. We prayed each day and helped our neighbors. However, despite our respect for the Church, we had never had a religious wedding. I think the importance of the sacrament of Marriage was hidden for us by the way weddings were experienced by most of our compatriots.

You have to see weddings in Africa! Feasts are prepared, and hundreds of people are invited. The poorer a couple is, the more they feel obliged to prepare a grandiose feast. Some of them put together such expensive parties that a few days after the wedding, they are hard-pressed simply to find enough food for themselves. It's completely absurd.

Léontine and I were satisfied with a ceremony in Bouaké, which was led by Fr. Pasquier, in the presence of three missionary sisters from Notre Dame des Apôtres, whom we rewarded with five jars of sweets. This wedding didn't cost us much! But we received the sacrament, which was all that mattered to us. We didn't even inform our families, who stayed in Benin. They learned about our wedding during the parish announcements at the end of Mass. But they understood our reasons. We were rather proud that after that, Fr. Pasquier often cited this wedding, which was so simple, as an example in his sermons.

AMIDOU

It stretched out its two antennae toward me. This is how ants talk. But it saw that I didn't understand and went back in the other direction. It went down my index finger toward the back of my hand. These little animals are always in such a rush! I had been having fun with this one for a long time. I walked it along my arm. I put obstacles in its way a hundred times with my fingers. But with the inexorable determination of its species, it always got around them. It made me feel good to see its vitality and sense the stinging sensation caused by its tiny feet on my skin. This reminded me that life, with its fevered and hectic rhythm, continued beyond my chain's radius. Being attached to my tree, I felt there was no more time to waste.

While thinking about this, I contemplated my ant, which was leaving the circle beyond which I could no longer go. If I stretched out my hand as far as possible with the chain around my neck, I could reach it with the tips of my fingers. No, it was over. It went further away. It left the small circle of my universe.

6

TO NICOLE'S RESCUE

It was 1982. While the members of St. Camillus were praying together at the hospital one day, our Hail Marys were interrupted by the periodic shouting of a patient. This was not surprising in a hospital. But this was a young boy's shout. It tore my heart out. When we finished saying the Rosary, I went to see a doctor I was very familiar with.

"What's the matter with this young patient who's making so much noise? Are you going to take care of him?"

"We can't!"

"Does he have an incurable illness?"

"No, his leg is fractured in several places, but the operation is too complicated, and his family doesn't have any more money. I think he'll be fine, but he'll have a limp."

"And if you had the money?"

"Then he could walk again. But where will you find the money? Antiseptics and casts—all that isn't free, you know!"

Yes, I knew that. I knew that if you have an accident in Africa and nobody comes to rescue you, those who drive by are required to let you die on the side of the road. If you have enough money on you to be taken care of, then you can be saved. Otherwise, you'll die. I knew that even those who go to the hospital aren't sure of being operated on. If they don't have enough money to cover an operation, they'll die. The hospital pharmacy is barred by a solid lock that you can open only after having paid the bill for the medicine and equipment that you need.

But I was incapable of leaving this young boy there. He was as small as a shrimp—like me when I was his age—and full of life. He didn't understand what was happening to him and was crying beside his devastated mother.

I went to see the members of St. Camillus. We reached into our pockets, and the little guy's leg was saved. It was so simple and logical that I couldn't, in truth, see how we could have acted otherwise. From that moment on, in addition to providing festive meals, we started to collect money for those who couldn't pay for operations they needed.

One morning, I came upon a pregnant woman who had died on the operating table. I saw a young doctor who was sitting near her. He was staring at the floor, as if there was something hidden under it. He looked up at me. His eyes were wet. He explained to me: "The pregnant woman came, and the delivery didn't go well. A C-section should have been prepared. But I wasn't there. We have all we need here to do it! But these are poor people. Nobody in the woman's family had any money to pay for the operation. I wasn't even called. And I can't blame the nurses who let her die there. They were only following the hospital's orders."

Despite my sadness at that moment, the doctor's tears reassured me. I've seen a lot of health-care providers become insensitive. It's as if they are clothed in armor in the face of everything that looks like empathy. This doctor wasn't part of that group.

I told him, "If you have a case like this one, call me. We can always find a solution with our St. Camillus friends."

"But, Grégoire, it was two o'clock in the morning."

"Don't worry about it!" I replied.

"What? You don't even have a phone!"

This is how I became the owner of one of those instruments that were appearing in Bouaké. It was the 1980s. It was a corded phone, of course, not one of those devices that clutter my pockets now. As of that date, I became something of a fireman. I knew I could be called in the middle of the night, and that if I got up, I could save a life!

One night, the phone rang. It was the doctor who had been so upset near the operating table. He had a new case—a single mother-to-be who had no money and needed a C-section—just like the preceding one.

I replied: "Tell them that Grégoire will come right away, and start the operation. We must not waste a minute!" When I arrived in the hospital, a nurse explained that the operation had already started. The doctor had only to give my name in order for the infirmary's janitor to open the hospital pharmacy doors. Reassured, I went home to sleep for a few hours.

I returned to the hospital with Léontine in the wee hours. The doctor welcomed us. He was radiant with joy. He immediately took us to see the young mother and her infant, who was sleeping peacefully. God is really good to His servants! He told me in no uncertain terms that our actions saved two lives.

God is really good, but He doesn't offer us an easy path. He honors us by letting us share His Cross.

One day, a mother in the hospital burst in on our prayer group. She begged for help. The doctors had just told her they couldn't do anything for her daughter Nicole. She was fifteen years old and had a heart problem. I went to go see the young girl, who was very weak. She explained her illness to me. There was no way to treat it there. Her case was too complicated. She would have to be sent to the cardiology services in a hospital in Abidjan. But it was very expensive: it would require a sum of a million and half CFA francs. It might as well have been said that it was completely impossible, even with St. Camillus's help. But I refused to stand idly by at Nicole's bedside, with her mother beside her. I said to the mother: "Don't lose hope. I'm going to go see the bishop. He may be able to do something for your daughter."

The bishop received me very kindly. He was already acquainted with St. Camillus, but he replied that he couldn't raise the amount I was asking for. Perhaps announcements could be made to the parishioners? In the meantime, he suggested that I go to the prefect.

So I went back on the road, and the prefect received me as kindly as the bishop did. He also appreciated the work I was doing at St. Camillus. But when I told him the amount I needed, he stared in amazement. He told me: "I don't have this money! You should go see the mayor."

The mayor was just as friendly as the others, but he couldn't give me the amount. He said to me: "If you find an ambulance, I'll pay for the gas and transportation costs, but what you're asking me for is impossible."

In short, I left this round with the equivalent of a container of gas and the authorization to call on the parishioners' solidarity. I was determined to use both. Then I started touring the parishes, opened a donation box for Nicole, and made my announcement at the end of the Masses. Word of mouth works well. Now a lot of people knew Nicole's name. I was even asked to make an announcement for her on television, but for that, it was required that I make known the exact amount of funds to be raised.

There was no longer any need to procrastinate. Nicole was sent to Abidjan in an ambulance that was loaned by the hospital's director and with the expenses paid by the mayor. The diagnosis cut like a knife. In addition to her heart problem, Nicole's lungs were infected. Even the doctors in Abidjan couldn't do anything—nothing, at least, from a medical point of view. We asked all the parishes and prayer groups we knew to pray for Nicole. Every day, I expected to receive a call telling me it was over.

Despite such an uncertain outcome, I didn't regret that St. Camillus rallied together for this kid's future. By moving Heaven and Earth, despite the gravity of this case, we participated in breaking the spirit of fatality that weighed on patients. Many people felt that the poor couldn't be saved—that it wasn't worth the struggle. Healthy children who suffered from illnesses or accidents from time to time and could be put back on their feet with modern medicine were instead abandoned every day for financial reasons! In the case of Nicole—who had a severe pathology, which was hard to treat even by the best doctors and those who were the best equipped—simple common sense would have dictated that we not waste our strength. But this isn't what we did, and by our efforts, we reminded our compatriots that everyone is precious in God's eyes—that God knows the number of hairs on the head of the least poor person.

At the hospital a few days later, I saw Denise, who had gotten involved with the St. Camillus group. As usual, she was carrying her pail of water and towels, which she used to wash the patients who didn't have parents to care for them. She came to tell me I had gotten a call. She was in shock. She told me: "The doctor who is taking care of Nicole has been redoing scans and ultrasounds for a week, and he always gets the same result. Nicole is healed! He doesn't understand. I think it's a miracle."

I believed it too. What else could we believe? That it was an extraordinary coincidence? It was so extraordinary that we had to consider it miraculous.

Nicole returned to Bouaké fully recovered from her illness. I hastened to introduce her to the bishop in order for him to bless her. Nicole's story made the rounds in Bouaké and went even beyond. Despite her healing, we continued to receive donations. But none of them was wasted. Every day, there were sick people who needed care and didn't have the money to pay for it. Once again, this adventure showed me that God was in charge. We must not worry about counting costs but must simply listen and love.

The St. Camillus Association got more money and became more famous with the Nicole affair. We were often called to help sick people who didn't have the money for their operations. In the cases that were reported to us, I was revolted to see the poverty of the people who were brought to us. I hadn't imagined the extent of their poverty or the mercenary logic that we should not treat those who didn't have the money for treatment.

St. Camillus was called on in the case of a little boy who had accidentally opened his abdomen with a knife. His intestines spilled to the outside. If nobody paid for his surgery, he'd remain like that! We, of course, took care of him, and the story for this boy ended well, but what if we hadn't been there?

I've also often seen serious cases—people in comas—and have been told: "There's no longer any need to spend any more on them. It would cost too much." But these are words I can no longer hear. Even if there are a hundred other sick people, I can't leave one out. Often, people I'm told are "incurable" wake up and leave in good health!

AMIDOU

It was morning. I felt strong, as in the days when I was leaving for a day of work in the fields. But the chain was still around my neck. The energy I felt circulating in me exasperated me. What was the point? Why was my heart still beating in my chest? Why was I breathing? I started to dig. I dug like an animal among the hard serpents of roots that were sinking into the ground. I was pleased to smell the freshness of the deep earth. It was a very long job, but that wasn't a problem. I had time—much too much time, in fact. The ground resisted, but I crumbled it with my fingers and nails and then threw it behind me. There were other roots under the roots. I uncovered a whole underground network. But there wasn't anything else. Perhaps if I dug deeper?

7

SERVING THOSE WHO ARE "IMPURE"

We started taking care of street children at the end of the 1980s. They had a bad reputation, but that was based on ignorance. I never had a problem with them—quite the contrary. They were so happy to receive a little help and attention that they treated St. Camillus's members with the greatest respect. You had to see the scene. The kids were gathered around me. They found a chair for me to sit on. It wasn't in very good shape. I was afraid one of its legs would break, but they were pleased with it. Thus, I was enthroned as a king of beggars in the middle of a group of kids who were sitting in a circle on the floor, and I distributed to each of them a plastic bag containing seasoned rice, which Léontine had prepared. We were a few hundred yards away from the St. Camillus Hospital—on a vacant lot between houses and plantations. It was the meeting place of these street children, who were quietly waiting to be served in turn.

They were usually good kids. But they were so poor that they were forced to beg—even to steal. I knew I didn't have the means to resolve their problems, but I brought them a meal. I started to know them. There were orphans and also runaways who came from families that were, let's say, complicated. Lord, there's so much misery that we don't suspect!

Helping the sick in the St. Camillus Hospital is like pulling a strand off a ball of yarn. As you help people, others come. There are other needs. But thank God, we find the resources to help them as we discover them. I don't make a plan. I don't develop anything. I follow a plan that has been created by someone else. This was how, while relieving small and big miseries, I discovered the lepers' situation.

Lepers are called the "impure ones," but, thanks to the work of several associations, Raoul Follereau's in particular, people's minds are changing. The medical profession now knows that leprosy is not a curse but an illness that isn't very contagious and that, above all, it can be treated. However, lepers are still living on the sidelines. They scare people. I'm attracted to them as I was attracted to the elderly people in my childhood, for I see that they need companionship. In fact, they need more than companionship. They need medical care. But what they suffer from the most is having society treat them as pariahs.

I got to know Véronique and Étienne, two lepers who were living in miserable conditions. Both were small and emaciated, like old wood. Étienne only had stumps of fingers on his right hand. Véronique had spots on her face and an ear that was damaged by the illness. They spent most of their time in a vacant house—away from the outside world. They scrounged for water and odds and ends to eat. Of course they welcomed the meals that St. Camillus prepared with pleasure, but they were both honored and frightened when I offered to bring the meals to their home. It was in this shelter of bricks that I assessed their misery—material, of course, but emotional, above all. Daylight didn't enter their house. They didn't want to be seen. Nobody knew them.

I went to see them from time to time. We talked about God and the upcoming Easter holiday. I perceived their sadness. They no longer had a family and would have to celebrate the Resurrection all by themselves. So I invited them to come to my house. Later, I did the same thing with other abandoned lepers, and since there were too many to fit my car, I chartered a bus that would bring them to my house. As is often the case, the small act of inviting a couple to the house took on rather large dimensions. Fortunately, Léontine shares my faith!

On Easter Day, I had some Italian friends from St. Camillus come for lunch at my house. The association started to be known by people in Europe, where we were raising money to help us in our mission. Among those who came for lunch was a priest who was visiting my country. While we were all talking together, the bus arrived in front of the house. There was a knock at the door. Léontine opened it, and the next moment, about forty lepers swamped the place. Some were missing fingers, feet, or a whole leg. The poor priest who, the moment before, had been chatting amiably with us, suddenly thought he was being thrown into the middle of a Court of Miracles. The lepers greeted our Italian friends to the best of their ability. Some magnificent smiles lit up their faces, many of which were ravaged by the disease. One of them exclaimed: "Grégoire, Léontine, Christ is risen!" The meal that followed was a bit odd but also festive and full of joy. It was impossible to know who was happier—they or I. The priest whom I involuntary put to the test still recalls this moment and often cites it in his sermons.

In the early days of St. Camillus in Bouaké in Côte d'Ivoire, I didn't have much time to return to my native country to see my family. However, I was worried about Mama. I was her only child, and, above all, she had no faith. So I was very happy when I heard that she decided to enter the catechumenate. In 1987, we went to the Holy Land together, and she was baptized in the Jordan River.

THEY ARE LIVING IN CHAINS

A few years later, she died, and a lot of friends from St. Camillus were kind enough to attend her burial. I recognized Étienne among them. I recall his fingerless hand at the time of the collection; he reached into his pocket to try to grab a coin. He who was so poor. It was impossible not to make the connection with the widow that the Gospel of St. Mark talks about (12:41–44). Étienne, like the widow, didn't give much, but, commensurate with his small savings, what he gave was huge. Sick people and little people really are our teachers in the Faith!

CHRISTIAN

There were only three months left before the test, and this frightened me. I was a good student, and I worked hard, but so many things depended on this diploma. In my small studio in Bordeaux, I often remembered my departure from Benin. All my extended family and some friends contributed for me to study in France and get my degree in mathematics. Everyone said I was a brilliant student, that my grades were excellent, and that I was serious. I'd soon come back with my diploma, and I'd be able to become an engineer. Then I would reimburse all those who helped me. But for now, I was still in this small studio with my stack of books. I wasn't happy here. I didn't know anyone. I didn't have any friends, I missed my country, and I was tired of feeling this pressure. I couldn't wait for the time to go by and for this test to be given, so I could finally get it over with!

8

I WAS A PRISONER, AND YOU VISITED ME

St. Camillus was growing. I still had my tire repair garage and my printer. All that was going well. My view of the world that surrounded me was changing. A lot of misery that had escaped me up until then jumped out at me.

Often after Mass, I saw a man who held out his hand for alms while he looked at the ground. He was very thin, but he didn't look sick or unhealthy. I noticed, however, that he had a lot of scars, and very few parishioners gave him alms. After seeing him several times, I decided to ask Fr. Pasquier about him.

"Father, I see a young man who's begging for money every Sunday, although he doesn't look sick. Do you know what's wrong with him?"

"He was a prisoner and was released. But now he's living here with no ties, and he's completely isolated."

"Where does he come from?"

"He comes from the prison camp. The unfortunate thing is that he doesn't even have the money to go back to his family. He's trying to save to return to Abidjan."

There were two big prisons in Bouaké — the civil prison and the prison camp. The prisoners are judged in Abidjan — about 250 miles from here—and then sent here. When they are released, they don't have any money. They are given only their exit ticket. This is why they stagnate. I thought that St. Camillus would be able to help them go back home, where they could have a chance to have a normal life again.

Léontine supported me, as usual. On the other hand, many of St. Camillus's members were dead set against this idea! "We're not going to help those who steal from us and kill us!" I replied with the Gospel: "I was in prison, and you visited me" (see Matt. 27:36). I called the prison's director, who, to my great surprise, was very supportive of a visit from a St. Camillus representative.

Thus, a few days later, I went to the prison camp to talk with the director about the possibility of coming to help the prisoners who were leaving the place. I knew the premises, without ever having passed through the door. During my trips, I often went in front of the high surrounding wall, which was indistinctly painted yellow and topped with barbed wire. But on that day, for the first time, I went in by the prison gate, which closed ponderously behind me, and entered a crazy, infernal world.

The prison, which, on the outside, looked like an official building, was outdated and in a state of unimaginable disrepair. Everything there was dirty and worn out. Heaps of garbage were piled against the leprous walls. The dusty ground was dug with rough gullies that were supposed to drain the rain. The dirt in it formed dams, and huge rats could slip through. The guards were tired and dazed. The assault rifles they carried on their shoulders were the only objects there that were in good shape.

The prisoners seemed to be immersed in another world. I didn't feel any hostility. Most of them didn't notice my presence. Some stared at me as if they were seeing through me. They were living like animals and were dazed by the heat and by idleness. At first, I didn't understand what I was seeing. I didn't understand what all these prisoners were doing there, tightly packed together. Then I realized that they were bunched up in the yard's only shadowy areas. It was morning, and the sun was getting higher and higher. As the day went on, the shadow dwindled. They weren't particularly mistreated by the guards, yet they suffered like the damned in this small hell. Their instruments of torture were the sun and other prisoners. There were a lot of them—too many for the space that was allocated to them.

I tried to picture the life of a man I saw there. He was about as old as I was, and he stared at me without seeing me. His T-shirt merged with his skin, and I could make out the pattern of his ribs underneath. His skin was no longer black but gray. It started to resemble the color of the dust that invaded everything during this dry season. I felt, looking at him, that he would soon disappear and merge with the yard's clay dirt. He was sitting on the ground, among the other prisoners, with nothing more to do than suffer and wait for lunch, which was the day's only meal. For a while, I didn't understand why the prisoners huddled together so tightly in their dormitory's shade. Some could find shelter inside rather than huddle together outside.

The guard saw that I was looking at the dormitories and said to me, "Come." He used the barrel of his rifle to clear a path through the prisoners. He did this without malice, like a breeder who clears a path in the midst of his cows by pushing them with a staff. And the prisoners weren't offended. They rose and made way for us with the same calm resignation as bovines. As soon as we went by, they took up the exact same places they had before. Each square centimeter of this yard was a dearly acquired treasure.

I entered the dormitory and couldn't make anything out. The heat, which was painful on the outside, was intolerable here, under the sheet-metal roofs. I was literally cooking. The bunk beds were unbelievably filthy. The smells pervaded everything. I felt that I was being filled with them—with odors of sweat, urine, and mold, and the blocked latrines that stank up the air. The guard explained that the prisoners slept in groups of three per bed. Those who arrived less than a year ago had to sleep on the ground against each other. They regularly changed sides during the night. It was impossible to sleep well in these conditions. This explained in part why they looked so dazed—never completely asleep or awake.

I started to get used to the darkness. But the heat was making me dizzy. I asked the guard to let me go out, and he led me outside. I understood why no prisoner wanted to stay inside. The sheet-metal roofs transformed the dormitories into an oven. The sun had now risen. There was no longer shade for everyone. The ones who were in the sun covered their faces with pieces of cardboard. The director arrived in the yard and called to me: "Come see!" I was unable to return to reality.

He explained the situation that I had discovered with horror. He talked to me about his management problems, the space issues, and the establishment's chronic overpopulation. One building that was planned for two hundred prisoners held five hundred of them.

Then he took me to the prison's infirmary. I saw several sick people who were handcuffed. They were chained to their beds. This made no sense for a lot of them, for they barely had enough strength to stand. I assumed they were treated like this in accordance with some obscure rule. I asked, without too much hope, if they were entitled to medical treatments, but evidently they were not—unless a member of their family was concerned about their fate and paid for their treatment. But that was rather rare, for prison was a terrible disgrace. People preferred to hide the fact that there were prisoners among their family members. The only way out for those with serious illnesses was the "prison cemetery," which was a very pompous name for a big hole in the ground dug by an excavator. Once a body was thrown in the bottom, sand was spread on it and, in this way, the tomb for the next person was ready.

The prisoners who were considered dangerous were confined to two-seater cells. There were seven or eight of them there. They wore chains all the time. The chains dug into their skin, like those iron rings sometimes left around a tree trunk. They were a part of them. Their faces were swollen and dug with deep marks, for they hit each other with the chains in order to create their own space and to avoid being attacked. It was as if their hands, which could be used to work and create, were amputated by these chains. They could no longer even strike each other with them.

A bell rang to announce the noon meal. The dazed crowd no longer existed. It was a frenetic herd fighting and jostling with one another to get to the pot to have their cardboard boxes or cans filled.

The cooks put rice wastes and peelings in their "soup." None of it was really substantial. What was being served to these men wouldn't be served even to a dog. I felt a terrible weight on my shoulders. There was too much misery. For too long we had failed to consider these people human beings.

This visit was like an uppercut to the liver. I was stunned. I couldn't get over the meanness men were capable of showing toward other men. I couldn't save them. But I could make sure that, from time to time, they had a meal that was worthy of its name.

I went to see the prosecutor, who was saddened by the state of the prison as I described it to him. He couldn't do much, but he agreed to have St. Camillus enter the prison to provide material aid.

Then I went to tell the St. Camillus members what I had seen. They were incredulous. And when I offered to prepare prisoner meals, I was told it was madness. To listen to them, these prisoners only got what they deserved! Luckily, some of them consented to follow me, and we agreed to line up some pots again to cook meals.

On the same evening of this trying day, someone broke into my car and stole my radio. I was told: "You see, you want to take care of thieves, and look at what they give back to you!" Once again, I heard about the "evil eye." I was tired of those stories. Yet, luckily, I had no doubts; I had to do something for these people. The St. Camillus members and I prayed for them with Léontine. Then I got busy cooking for the prisoners.

Despite the first cold reception that I had gotten about my project, many of the St. Camillus members and priests and parishioners whom Fr. Pasquier encouraged came to help me. We soon knocked on the prison door with huge pots full of rice and fish with tomato sauce. We had planned to give them to the prisoners as well as their guards.

Needless to say, we were immediately accepted. I think that, above and beyond the food, the prisoners were struck to see that we had prepared this festive dish for them as we would have done for ourselves. We went to great lengths. We put some spices in it and presented it well. For the first time in a very long time, these unfortunate people were treated like men. The members of St. Camillus who made the trip with me were immediately committed to the cause of these prisoners. None of them would ever say again that they "got what they deserved."

We agreed to offer them festive meals and to pay for the trips of those leaving prison to return to their families. We then visited the women's prison, where we discovered a situation that was almost as terrible as the men's. There were children among them. Some of the women were locked up pregnant or with young children. But there were also orphans who were put there for having committed minor offenses or simply for having been found undocumented.

We discovered Joseph among them. He was a very thin nine-year-old from Burkina Faso who turned out be a resourceful little guy without a family. He had secretly entered Côte d'Ivoire by hanging under a train. (Côte d'Ivoire has a better economic situation than Burkina Faso.) The boy managed to earn a little money by selling ice water on the streets. One day, he put down his things and his money to play ball with some other kids. When he went back to look for his things, he found that they had disappeared. A woman, believing she was doing the right thing, advised him to go see the police. He did so, but when the police officers discovered that Joseph was undocumented, he was sent to prison. He told me his story, and I didn't understand how this could happen—that a kid could be thrown into prison in this way. And you had to see what a prison it was! I explained his case to the director, and Joseph was released.

As the members of St. Camillus came to know the prison, we discovered other Josephs. It was hard to believe that simple kids, who hadn't done anything in particular, got locked up, with no anticipated release date. They were simply left there to wait and perish. Yet neither the guards nor the director were sadistic.

The essence of the problem was that the prison was a kind of garbage can: a place where they got rid of not only dangerous people but also people whom they didn't know what to do with—people who were disturbing, for one reason or another. These undocumented kids were a problem for the administration, which had surely received strict instructions for migrants, and rather than coming to help them or simply releasing them, they clearly preferred to put them in the prison's "big garbage can."

We managed, with St. Camillus, to organize festive meals and have some child captives like Joseph released. Above all, we set up a solution for those who were leaving the prison to return home. The administration gave them a "trip paid by St. Camillus" ticket. They could return to Abidjan with this door opener. I wanted to pay tribute to the transportation companies that lent us a hand by offering a spot in their bus for 2,000 CFA instead of the usual 5,500 CFA. We managed, with a little goodwill, to improve the fate of the prisoners a bit.

CHRISTIAN

I don't know when this started. But I gradually became more certain that I was going to fail the test. I tried to imagine how the news of my failure would be received in my country. I would not be rejected, of course, but it would be such a disappointment for all those who believed in me and invested their money in my education. At this point, I got a grip of myself and returned to my worktable. But mysteriously I grew incapable of working. Everything tired me out. I even had a hard time getting out of my bed in the morning.

The test was in ten days, and there were no more classes. This time was given to us to review, but this period was terrible for me. For one thing, I had few contacts here.

I saw that it wasn't good to keep shutting myself away, so I tried getting out a little. But I felt stupid wandering in this city that was full of people who knew where they were going and what they were doing. I did my little shopping, which was always the same—pasta and tomato sauce. If Mama saw what I was eating here, she would be indignant. Nothing had any more taste. I ate at my desk, where my lessons were messily piled up.

This wasn't like me. I was swimming in the fog. I was so tired and sad. I felt that my life's whole horizon was summed up in these two words: *fatigue* and *sadness*.

9

THE FIRST "LUNATIC"

It was 1992. The years had gone by in this way. I didn't overcome my misery, but I dared to face it. I fought it. The sacraments were a daily comfort in this fight. In them, I looked for Jesus, who saves us. I didn't, however, expect to meet Him in the flesh as I saw Him one day.

It was one of those full days that were interspersed with meetings. I sped along on one of Bouaké's congested roads. I continued to drive fast, as before. This was a flaw in my personality that I had never corrected. Figures of my company's progress no longer preoccupied my mind; those of St. Camillus's evolution did. I was returning from one of my prison visits when a terrible traffic jam completely blocked my way. As an old hand at Côte d'Ivoire roads, I knew that it wasn't a simple bottleneck. I could stay stuck there for a long time, and I looked for a backup solution. There was a little alley that would just barely let my good old Peugeot 505 go through. I pushed my accelerator really hard and headed in that direction in order to escape the traffic.

Pedestrians were clogging the way. I slowly moved forward until I came across a completely naked, haggard man who was crossing the street. After he reached the other side of the street, I saw him start searching a garbage can. He was carefully turning over the garbage and looking for any bit of food that might be stuck to the bottom of a dented can or cardboard box. My heart was turned upside down.

A truth suddenly struck me. This man was Jesus! He's the one we put in gold monstrances and whom we adore in our churches while raising incense to Him. He was there looking for bits of spoiled food in the bottoms of rusty cans amid the stench of people's household garbage. I continued on my way and was deeply disturbed.

After my workday, while I was lying on my bed, the thought of this man kept nagging me. I realized that there had always been men like him in front of me. Many years ago, I almost ran one down in my car. He was a poor wretch, who was also completely naked and missing an ear. People in Africa say that such people are possessed or bewitched. They are afraid of them. They don't like them to get close to normal people. They like to throw stones at them.

The guy I saw wasn't dangerous. He was simply sick—a "lunatic," as we often say—someone who's mentally ill. If he had a liver disease or a broken leg, his family would take care of him, but since he's mentally ill, they let him wander on the streets. They are afraid of him. Most of the time, we prefer not to think about the mentally ill, and if we do, we tell ourselves that what they are experiencing isn't serious, for they are "in their own world" and indifferent to the outside world. But this is obviously false—completely false! They suffer, just as everyone suffers from being alone and not having enough to eat or any shelter. From that day on, "lunatics" no longer left my head. I had glimpsed the depths of their distress, and I couldn't take my eyes off it. I felt dizzy.

While I was crossing the streets in Bouaké on the evening after my encounter, I wondered how to meet them. I had to understand these people. How did they survive? What did they need? I didn't really know. In fact, nobody seemed to know. Yet I knew a lot of medical personnel. It's very strange that the people who are always under our noses are invisible; in fact, I looked for one that night and didn't find one. I wanted to try to follow one and talk to him. But it was no use pacing up and down the streets where I had already seen some "lunatics." It was as if they had vanished.

The night was falling when I discovered one. He was dressed only in shorts and was sidling along the walls, as if to stay hidden. I didn't know how to approach him. I had brought a bottle of fresh water and a cup, but I didn't dare go and offer it to him. He seemed scared and was moving in the shadow of the buildings and looking around him. He saw me, glanced at me suspiciously, and continued on his way. I followed him from afar, with my bottle and cup, which encumbered my hands. This man who was wandering and whom I was trying to follow to find out where he slept was Jesus. I no longer had any doubt about this, and yet I didn't have the courage to go unhesitatingly toward him to meet him. He disappeared at the corner of an alley. I wasn't able to see how he had lost me. He wasn't anywhere!

So I went back home, dejected. How could we help people who are so suspicious of us? Why is there such an abyss between them and us?

Over the next few days, the case of these men continued to trouble me. I noticed one who was wandering near my home, and again, I followed him with a bottle of fresh water and a cup. I understood that communicating with these people would take time. This man was completely out of it. He was naked, wandering, and talking to himself. I followed him from afar. He didn't notice me. After a while, I saw him stop. I hid in the shade. He looked in front of him, in back of him, and on all sides. Then I saw him crouch down and disappear into the ground! I no longer saw him. After a while, I decided to look closer. I understood. The man took refuge in the one of those big gutters that are meant to collect the torrential rains that fall on us. Unfortunately, the gutters are so blocked by the garbage that we don't even see them anymore—like this man who sensed that we didn't like to see him. He felt that nobody appreciated his presence, and so he tried to take his place amid the garbage that clutters our streets. But I had a thought: the garbage that we throw in the gutters doesn't disappear; it accumulates and pollutes our lives. This man didn't stop being a man because he took his place amid garbage and lost all dignity.

I went back home feeling stunned—as if crushed by the misery that I'd only just glimpsed.

I tried again on the following night. I noticed one of these "lunatics" who was sleeping in a little wasteland that wasn't far from my home. He was completely naked, and I brought him some clothes—a pair of pants and a T-shirt that should have fit him. I went by the broken fence that separated his universe from the street. An unceremonious crumpling of cardboard greeted me. The man lived there. He got up and rolled his frightened eyes. I told him: "Don't be afraid. I don't want to hurt you! I simply came to give you some clothes." But he ran off, as frightened as if I had been a lion! I was distraught. I put the clothes on the cardboard that he used as a mattress and left very sad.

I went back the next day, and when I went by the fence that marked out his little kingdom, I once again heard the unceremonious crumpling of cardboard. My man was there. He was dressed in the clothes I had left there the day before. This time, he didn't flee, but he did something almost worse. He looked at me furiously. His right hand, which was raised high, held a big stone. He stammered: "If you come any closer, I'm going to hit you! You're going to die!"

I was careful not to go near him. But I stayed in front of him with my water bottle and cup. I replied: "It's warm. I brought you some water. Don't you want to drink a little?"

He repeated his hasty and menacing sentence and was stuck in his defensive attitude. His muscles were tight. He was ready to strike.

I answered him: "I don't want to hurt you at all. I'm trying to help you."

But he repeated his threat over and over again. It seemed that this was the only sentence that he had left to communicate. I saw that nobody had spoken kindly to this man for a very long time. He must have lived through some atrocious experiences. I stayed in front of him and waited for him to relax. But this didn't happen. We stayed four steps away from each other. After perhaps about ten attempts, I decided to risk moving forward. I took one step and then two steps, under the furious eye of the man who was still waving the stone above his head. Halfway there, I stooped to put the bottle and cup down, at the risk of being hit.

But nothing happened. I got back up and moved back again two steps. I told him: "You have nothing to fear from me. I'll return to see you. I want to help you."

And this is what I did.

LÉONIE

I no longer know how old I am. I was sixteen years old when I ran away, after having gnawed at my rope. But after that, there weren't really any more weeks, months, or years. Days followed days—always with the same obsessions: finding shelter, finding something to eat and drink, and avoiding men who wanted to harm me. Sometimes I made friends with a woman who lived on the streets like me, but each time, this ended badly. In fact, the only real companionship were the voices that spoke in my ear.

Why did they have to be so mean? Most of the time, they told me I was a bad girl and that I made Mama cry. But she's the one who tied me to a stake. And the voices told me to leave and never come back. They preached what was true and false. They contradicted each other. In fact, they had only one consistent pattern. They did what they could to make me feel bad.

10

THE WORLD OF "LUNATICS"

These "lunatics" that I approached started to win me over. They must have told themselves that I looked like them since I walked with my fresh water and cup every night with no apparent goal. I managed to strike up conversations with many of them.

This started with the one whom I clothed and who had threatened me with a stone. As I had told him, I went back to see him. This time, when I went by the fence, he asked me: "Do you have water?" It was obviously not very polite, but the man no longer had a stone in his hand. He rose above me, standing on his boxes, and scrutinized me. As on the day before, I placed the bottle two steps in front of him. I added a bag of rice with tomato sauce that Léontine had prepared. He took two steps, grabbed the water and the food, and went back to his place. He crouched down and started to drink and eat in front of me. He was obviously thirsty and starving. He became friendly. The sentence he had repeated over and over again: "If you get closer, I'll hit you! You're going to die!" was not the only one he knew how to say. While eating, he said to me: "It's good. . . . I thought you were with them—that you wanted to capture me."

He was obsessed. He was sure that people in his native village, which was far away in the bush, wanted to harm him. This was why he lived here—shut away in the anonymity that the city provided.

In what he described to me, it was hard to separate reality from his delirium. He said that the people in his village had become bad, that they hurt him, and that they had even tied him to a tree with a very short chain, like a goat to its post. He talked about the "spirits" that spoke to him, about wandering along roads, and about heat and hunger. But over the course of our meetings, I discovered that idleness was what made him suffer the most. When he was in a good mood, he remembered that he was called "the vigorous one" in the village because he worked hard in the fields. But that was now a bygone era. He was no longer working and said he wasn't useful anymore.

I learned to speak to him and to others. They were all very suspicious and paranoid. At first, I thought it was because of their illness, which made them think everyone detested them, but I gradually realized this was only partially true. Everyone rejected them. People threw stones at them to keep them away. I managed to reach them little by little with my water and bags of rice. I understood that, in order for them to be trusting during the first meetings, they always had to have an exit. You couldn't get too close to them if you didn't know them—not because they were dangerous but because they were always afraid of a trap.

I was stunned by their numbers. I discovered that there was a "crossroads of lunatics" in Bouaké. There were more mentally ill people in this corner, for one reason or another, than in any other region. They didn't, however, communicate with each other. They were locked up in their world of mistrust and so avoided each other. Those who were "healthy" rejected the people in this place, like a huge dump. The families who could no longer bear the burden of one of these sick people took them there and abandoned them to their sad fate.

I couldn't leave them in this condition.

During the following St. Camillus meeting, I expounded on the case of the cognitively disabled. I told them there were people near us who were living in total destitution whom nobody was caring for and that all they needed was a little respect. My audience was attentive, but when I said this was about cognitively impaired people, I sensed that the group became discouraged.

I heard many of the members of the group sigh. Others were simply perplexed. After the meeting, one of the faithful, who was a pillar of the association, came to see me. She told me, "Grégoire, I understand that their fate is making you suffer. What you are offering is lovely, but it's unreachable. These people have sicknesses that make them dangerous and unpredictable. You shouldn't get involved in their lives! You're not a doctor and don't have the skills that are required for that. We already have enough work with the sick and with prisoners without adding this burden that's impossible for us to carry."

This generous Christian woman was talking reasonably. Moreover, she was the voice of what a lot of people were thinking. I understood them perfectly! Not long ago, I thought like them. A few months ago, if I had been asked to care for cognitively disabled people, I would have said no! But things had changed since then. I saw them. Above all, I saw Christ in them. I can't forget this vision. I loved them and wanted to help them.

Fortunately, the hesitation of my St. Camillus friends, which was completely normal, disappeared in the face of the reality of the mentally ill. When they rubbed shoulders with lepers, prisoners, and those we call "lunatics," their fears flew away, and the mutual aid work could start!

I increased the quantities of food that I organized for the patients. I prepared my rounds and started looking for solutions to their illnesses. At the time, I had no idea of the scope of the work I was about to undertake, and that was a good thing! Had I known this, I would have probably gotten discouraged. That's why I often recall this truth: I'm not the founder of the St. Camillus Association. Jesus is!

I discovered Étienne among the sick. He was a confused, shaggy young man with protruding ribs who was wandering in Bouaké. I often met him, and a relationship of trust was established between us. In addition to his mental illness, this young man was bothered by the big steel nuts he had put on his fingers—like rings. I assumed he thought they were beautiful. Far from it, for they were so tight that he could no longer remove them. He tried to do this in front of me but without success. His fingers were bizarrely swollen around his ring fingers, which were probably damaged. I couldn't leave him like that. We went to the garage to try some tools, but the problem wasn't obviously resolvable. How could we remove big steel nuts that clutched fragile fingers of flesh so tightly? We decided to secure one of the nuts in a vice in order to cut it out without having Étienne's hand move. He let it be done but looked nervously at his finger that was locked in a vice.

I reassured him and said: "Don't look. There are going to be sparks. We're going to remove the nut. It might make some noise, but we're not going to hurt you!"

Étienne understood. He trusted me, and as I picked up the circular saw, I hoped to deserve that trust. My plan was to notch the nut enough to be able to pull it apart. I began to do it. The saw made a terrible noise, but things started out well. My patient remained quite tame while I was notching the nut.

Suddenly, I heard him cry out in pain! I hadn't cut him, though. He shouted: "It's burning!" Evidently, the screw was heating up with the friction of saw on the steel. I should have thought of that! I removed the saw. After several fruitless attempts, we found a solution that worked. Once the nut was half cut—without letting the saw run for too long—I tightened it with the vice until it broke. Étienne was freed from the nuts, but, unfortunately, he never recovered the use of his fingers.

Thanks to the trust of Étienne and others, I understood the reality of a cognitive disability better. What I'm going to say may seem obvious, but such a disability is, first of all, an illness. We can treat it and sometimes even heal it by taking care of the patients and having the right medicine. Some people call me a "mental doctor," but that's completely false. I'm not a doctor. I stopped going to school when I was twelve years old! Nonetheless, in order to understand mental illness better, I did a two-month internship in the general hospital. I saw what doctors did in the intensive care unit. I became acquainted with neuroleptic medicine; they are astonishingly effective but often are not permanent. A lot of patients can lead a life that's almost normal as long as they regularly take their medicine. I discovered this in the 1990s, but thirty years later, I continue telling the patients: "Don't stop taking your medicine with the excuse that you're doing better! The illness hasn't left. It's simply sleeping."

One thing I wasn't expecting is that it turns out that many "lunatics" I talk to aren't suffering much. They have some quirks and wounds, of course, but the vast majority of those quirks and wounds come from their isolation, not from the illness. In the midst of the contempt of us "healthy people," they sleep poorly on the streets, are always on the lookout, and don't feel safe anywhere. Even someone who is completely healthy would develop mental illnesses in those conditions. In thinking about this, I started imagining an "asylum"—a place that would belong to them where they could feel good.

This is how the first reception center was created. The hospital lent us a former café where patients could go to get some food and medicine that St. Camillus paid for. Very soon, these premises were too small. The patients needed a place to rest and eat. I wanted a real guesthouse that would completely take care of them. The hospital's director, whom I talked to about this project, commended me to nobody less than Côte d'Ivoire's minister of health.

So I called the minister, who was cordial and understanding. He agreed to come help me with a 2,400-square-meter building plot that he donated to us on the grounds of the university hospital. This was a good fit, but we still needed to build our establishment!

We didn't have five francs to devote to this project. St. Camillus had already struggled to find the money to buy medicine and food. Fr. Allirand, the treasurer, told me that my project was generous but that we had to remain reasonable. But was it reasonable to leave these people without shelter?

In January 1994, despite everything, I went to see a mason to ask him to start building the walls. I dreamed of a chapel, a small free clinic, and a resting place. All of that started to spring up because, fortunately, people sent me donations. Thanks to them, I could pay the workers every month, although sometimes with a bit of a delay.

I knew moments of doubt. One week, the coffers were completely empty. Saturday was getting closer. There was a big Muslim feast coming up. Our workers were Muslim, and we couldn't leave them without paying them that week. It was much too important. I dwelled on the problem and was very worried. But while I was experiencing this moment of anguish, Hélène, a member of the association, gave me an envelope. She explained to me: "Someone gave me this for you. He didn't want to tell me his name." I opened it and found a bundle of bills. I couldn't believe my eyes. This bundle contained the exact amount I needed to pay the workers! There wasn't more or less than a franc. All my doubts flew away, and I thanked God, who showed me how much He was protecting us and blessing our work!

CHRISTIAN

Today was the day of the test, and I couldn't even get out of bed. I hadn't touched my notebooks or eaten for several days. I had a headache and was desperate. Perhaps, if I got out of bed now, I could still get to the examination room on time? 8:45. Not a chance. Even if I ran or broke the speed record, I couldn't take the test. It was going to start in fifteen minutes.

11

THE ST. CAMILLUS CENTERS

The chapel finally sprang up. Glory to God! It was immediately used by my patients, who often went there. They talked and rested in its shelter. We had prayer times. Fr. Allirand came to say Mass there, which most of the patients experienced as an event of the utmost importance. The room was full. There were friends of St. Camillus and all kinds of patients. Some lay on mats on the floor and slept during the service. It was a little strange, but they respected the altar that stood on a platform and didn't shout or make any noise.

While Father started the Consecration, I was happy to see these people's newfound peace. Many of them had difficult behaviors when they were on the streets. They were excessively suspicious and frightened or else in a state of delirious euphoria. They were quiet and calm here. While I was thinking about this, I saw one of the patients get up and start screaming. The little moment of peace quickly went away. But while I rushed toward him to try to calm him down, I saw a dozen "patients" crowd in toward him to talk to him. The crisis stopped as suddenly as it had started, thanks to those whom, until recently, I had described as "mentally ill people."

In fact, they asked nothing more than to come to the aid of one of their brothers. This is the best therapy we could dream of. These people whom we treat as garbage and whom we say are impossible to take care of are full of resources.

I note the case of Véronique among them. This older woman who wandered the streets in the grip of delusions of persecution was doing better since she started visiting the center. She still had a hard time reaching out to others and often tried to take up much of my time in talking to her and reassuring her.

This is how one day, while I was talking with her, as often happened, a young girl I had never seen arrived in the center. She was haggard and completely shaggy. She stood in front of the doorway looking lost. I apologized to Véronique: "I must go see this young girl. She doesn't dare come in." Véronique answered me immediately: "Give me a pair of scissors to neaten up this poor girl! I'm a good hairdresser!"

And this is what she did. While I was talking to the young girl, whom a friend of the association had led here, strands of her hair fell around us. I asked her what her name was and whether she was hungry or thirsty. She responded incoherently. She talked about the bush and said that she had been tied up. I saw marks of ropes on her hands. She must have pulled very hard to get free of them. This girl was still in shock. Despite her young age, she was considered to be a public danger and was treated worse than an animal. Her testimony confirmed some observations I had already made. It obviously happens that some mentally ill people who are considered to be dangerous are tied up like animals.

When I finished talking with her, Véronique started braiding the girl's hair. She was transformed! The wild child who was running away from the bush turned into a beautiful young girl before our eyes.

The St. Camillus Centers

We were outside, in front of the chapel. Several young girls started forming a circle around Véronique. They were very interested in her work. The hairdresser was so proud, and I was proud of her too! The work we were doing here was transforming hearts. I only had one wish: to make it grow! Later, the patients who could cook started working, and soon they made the meals for the prisoners in Bouaké. We wouldn't have gone very far without this collective endeavor and the willingness of the patients to participate in this work.

Some people I didn't know started bringing patients. These were often family members who no longer knew what to do with the patients. One morning, an elderly lady came to see me to tell me that we had to go find her son, Julien. I saw that she was uncomfortable, so I took her aside and asked her:

"What's the matter with your son? What did you do to him?"

"He's sick in the head and dangerous!"

"So you tie him up?"

"Yes, we can't let him go out. He's dangerous."

We so often attribute the word *dangerous* to mentally ill people! Most of the time, they are simply frightened.

"You never let him go out?"

"No, we can't. He's dangerous."

"How long has he been tied up like this?"

"For two years."

Tied up for two years!

I immediately left with this lady to see the one who would become my "first tied-up person." I drove quickly, as always, spurred on by the thought of this poor Julien who was living in shackles. From roads to trails, we arrived in a small village, where our arrival immediately drew a crowd.

I asked: "Where is Julien?" and got out of the car with my toolbox under my arm.

A moment later, I saw a little girl—she could not have been more than seven years old—who was holding a pickaxe that was bigger than she was. She rushed toward a little adobe shelter next to a house that was right in front of me. The little girl, with all the strength she was capable of, lifted the pickaxe above her head and struck the ground at the foot of a stake that was deeply driven into the ground. A chain, which went through a narrow loophole right into the adobe shelter, was connected to this stake. I saw the girl struggling energetically, but with little success, and I went into the shelter.

Julien was there. He was motionless in the small, dark room. The chain that went through the loophole was connected to a bracelet that clutched his right ankle. His left foot was also clamped, and a chain went through another loophole. It was also attached to a stake outside, at a point that was diametrically opposed to the first one. I now understood why the stakes were placed outside the room. That way, it was impossible for Julien to extract them. And since he was attached to two points, he had very little space to move in. This didn't allow him to dig in the clay wall to look for a way out. The only things he had within easy reach were a bowl of water and a pot to relieve himself. He hid his eyes since he was blinded by the light that I had let in by opening the door.

I heard the continuing noise of the pickaxe outside. The little girl was trying to unearth the stake.

I went up to Julien, who was still motionless, and I gently spoke to him: "We're going to get you out of here. I'm going to cut the chain, and you're going to come with me. We're going to take care of you." He looked at me without understanding. The bracelets on his ankles were too big for me to cut with my hacksaw. I'd need a vice and a circular saw. But I could cut the chain. It would still be better than to let it drag with us into the car. I attacked it, under the watchful eye of Julien and many of the villagers who crowded around us.

The little girl was no longer digging. She also joyfully looked at us and devoured us with her eyes. This was Julien's daughter. She had been waiting for this day for a long time. Julien was very calm. When the chain was broken, he submissively followed me, with his bracelets still on his foot. His daughter refused to let him leave, so we had to take her with her father.

Julien was only the first one of a long line of people in chains. His story with the disease ended well, for he regained his faculties and could later return to his village with his family. But I discovered that there were many who lived this way and whom nobody talked about it.

When I released another sick person, who was literally nailed to the ground, like Christ on the Cross, and rebuked the family for treating him that way, they answered me: "He's rotten and possessed!" And this poor man died soon after, but, for all that, he never stopped being a man, and he had a dignified death rather than the torment that was inflicted on him. However, this family was no worse than any other one. They acted like this because of their erroneous beliefs. They thought, like so many others, that mental illness had destroyed the person. Because mental illness attacks the brain, it prevents people from managing their emotions and communicating accurately. We often conclude that it has destroyed the person's intelligence and dignity. This is false. Therefore, our first job at St. Camillus is to educate people.

In this work, we must fight against superstitions that are solidly embedded. When I began to assess the abuses that were inflicted on the mentally ill, I discovered the dire reality of "prayer camps." These are centers that are managed by unstable pastors who claim to be fighting against demons. The mentally ill, who are considered to be possessed, are mistreated there.

Accordingly, I received a chilling call from the Benedictine sisters in Bouaké. They told me: "There's a prayer center next to our convent where sick people are mistreated. We hear them screaming!" It was on the outskirts of the city, right under our noses, so to speak. I went to the site. There were big pictures of Jesus and rather threatening slogans that mentioned the book of Revelation. I wanted to go in, but they wouldn't let me enter. I was furious and went to city hall to obtain the right to see what was happening in this prayer center.

The mayor sent an emissary with me to prove that I was going there with his authority. This time, they didn't dare push us back in the entrance hall, and we went into the prayer center. We saw sick people tied to poles in a yard in rows, like tomato plants. I heard furious shouting, and I rushed over to investigate. The pastor who was directing the center was standing on one of his victims. He struck him while shouting, "Get out, demon!" I was stunned and shouted: "If that's believing in God, it's not worth it, eh?" The emissary rose up and grabbed the pastor by the collar. He was even more furious than I was: "We're going to go to the courthouse. I'm going to testify. I'm going to look for the police right away!"

And that's what he did. The police arrived and took over the premises. There were about forty sick people there, and their chains were cut with a joyful jingle. The police sergeant came to me at the end of the operation. He was very uncomfortable: "But now, what are we going to do with these sick people?"

This was the question that bothered me as well. St. Camillus had to grow, and, as usual, we didn't yet have a plan. We simply needed to do this. So we worked on the construction of a new center.

It had not yet gotten off the ground when we learned about another terrifying matter. While a city was preparing for festivities to the north of the region, all the mentally ill people who were wandering on the streets were put in a garbage truck. Then the truck would unload its contents in the bush.

I immediately called the city's mayor to ask if he was aware of this matter. I was amazed that he not only knew what was happening but that he himself had issued those inhumane instructions. He explained: "I must clean up my city before the holidays. 'Lunatics' are a blot on the landscape. So, we take them away like garbage in a garbage truck."

I couldn't believe it! I told him: "Stop immediately! Send the truck to me in Bouaké. I'll take care of the sick people!" And the mayor, who was indifferent, replied: "Okay, they haven't yet been released into the bush. We'll send them to you."

The next day, the truck reached the St. Camillus Center in Bouaké. The drivers opened the rear trapdoor, as if they were making their usual rounds. A stench came from the dumpster. The "lunatics" were frightened and sticking to each other, and their hands were tied.

I got very angry with the drivers, who didn't understand my reaction: "You've tied their hands up as if they were criminals! You're the criminals! You're the ones who should be in the back in the heat and the stench!" The drivers indistinctly replied that the police had tied them up and that they were only driving the truck.

This is how we delegate, deny responsibility, and end up with the worst horrors. Neither the mayor, nor the police officer, nor the drivers thought about helping these poor people.

We had a lot of trouble managing to house and properly clothe those "lunatics." We tried to find their families and asked for

support everywhere that we could. Luckily, the St. Camillus network continued to grow. We found a new spot in Nimbo, on the
outskirts of Bouaké. St. Camillus had grown and was obviously
called to grow again.

CHRISTIAN

I don't know how I got home to the village. My village no longer looked like what it did before. It had become so small! I took a plane and went to France. When I flew over the desert and the Mediterranean, I felt as if I were conquering the world! But now, my universe was dramatically reduced. They said I had a brain disease. But I knew I had failed. I had a medical treatment and talked to a psychiatrist. But nothing could sever this strange sadness that took a hold of me in Bordeaux—like a bad spell. I only saw my failure where I grew up. It was always before my eyes.

12

FORMER PATIENTS AT THE HELM

More and more patients arrived in the St. Camillus centers in 1995. We had some cash-flow problems, but they were gradually resolved, thanks to the generosity of African, European, and Lebanese donors. Some of the patients went back to their families and villages. But we often had bad experiences with those. Many of those who needed to be treated discontinued their medicine and relapsed. Others slipped back into their shortcomings.

The example of Véronique and other recovering sick people like her were on my mind. I wanted to find a way to let patients who were getting better work in St. Camillus. In this way, we could keep them in a secure environment and give them a leg up so that they could get on with their lives. Very often, the mentally ill person feeds on the feeling of uselessness, which undermines his morale and prevents him from becoming self-confident.

It would be most efficient to have fields that could be cultivated. The majority of the patients had, like me, started their active lives by doing small jobs in the fields. That didn't require any specialized skills—only goodwill and courage. They had a lot of it to offer! This activity could be used to generate profits, and we could use some more money.

I found some land that would be perfect and was actually on sale—for thirty million CFA francs! I didn't have any money for it. On the other hand, I had friends, for St. Camillus now had faithful rich donors. Esper Badi was among them. He was a Lebanese Christian who had settled in Côte d'Ivoire and to whom I often spoke. He was an impressive businessman, and in addition to his professional activity, he had a heart of gold. I told him about my project. He approved my vision of things but warned me: "What you're undertaking will require some money—a lot of money. I can't bring it to you by myself. If you manage to buy this land, I'll pay for the fence you'll need to close off the land."

Like the twelve-year-old schoolboy I once was, I did my best, with some difficulty, to write a letter in which I explained to the owners that I'd like to acquire their land. With a little luck, seeing that it was for a good work, I was hoping they would reduce their price. But a week after sending my letter, I still had no reply. Maybe they hadn't received it. That happens. So I called on the phone, and a cheerful female voice answered me right away. I introduced myself:

"Hello. This is Grégoire. I wrote you about your land."

"Ah, yes, you want the land for St. Camillus. Is that right? You've created a magnificent work!"

"You know, I'm not the founder. Jesus is."

"We'd like to help you, Mr. Grégoire. [At that moment, I was waiting for her to add "but we can't because ..."] My husband and I have talked about it, and we'll give you the land. Come set it up as soon as you need it. I'm warning you that you'll have to do a lot of clearing!"

I couldn't believe my ears! They didn't want even one franc!

This is how the Dar-es-Salam ("fruit of providence" in Arabic) Center came into being in the northern part of Côte d'Ivoire in

1996. We offered training in agriculture and baking. The first convalescents, who were coming out of the Bouaké centers, were immediately sent there. We started cultivating corn, peanuts, and cassava. We also raised hens and hogs.

We now had an ophthalmological center in the hospital, and we made optical lenses. This didn't please private clinics, which spoke to the minister of health to accuse us of "dishonest competition." Fortunately for us, their timing was bad. The minister of health appreciated St. Camillus and snapped back at the accusers that they had better turn against the doctors who were being paid by the state and leaving to go work in private clinics! Later, another complaint was filed against me for "dishonest competition." Here again, the complaint was dismissed.

Some more serious attacks came from professional psychiatrists who estimated—quite rightly—that St. Camillus didn't have adequately trained staff or the physical conditions that were needed to take care of cognitively disabled situations. I replied: "Come bring them to us!" But when the conversation reached this point, it unfortunately came to a sudden end.

There were two psychiatric hospitals for the whole Côte d'Ivoire. This wasn't much. But some medical students who were majoring in psychiatry started to become interested in our work. One day, I brought over half a dozen of them so they could see what we were achieving in one of our brand-new farms that we were managing with the recovering patients. They were impressed by the extent of our undertaking. The center's new manager welcomed them on the premises. He explained that a lot of the land was still uncultivated but that there were already some plantations of yams, banana trees, and oil plants that were starting to grow. He paused to advise a group of about twenty young men who were clearing a parcel of forest with a cutter to prepare more plantations.

One of the students said to me: "I thought you had only a few staff members. How did you find these workers? Are they seasonal workers?"

I replied: "No! All those workers you see are patients. The center's manager is the only St. Camillus employee."

The manager piped up: "Incidentally, I'm a former patient as well!"

They all stared in amazement.

Then the student explained: "In school, they teach us not even to leave a pen within reach of a mentally ill patient. We give them only plastic place settings in the cafeteria. Yours have machetes as long as your arm!"

Their reaction made me laugh. "I don't have money to pay seasonal workers, so I ask the patients to work. By the way, it's part of their treatment. A patient who works feels useful again and is already almost healed!"

Very often, the problem with the mentally ill doesn't come from their bad will or that of their relatives. It's from a lack of confidence. The best example that was given to me was from a corner of the bush where Christian was wasting away. I discovered this intelligent, serious, and even brilliant young man with his foot tied to a huge trunk. He no longer saw anyone besides his mother, who came to clean him up and bring him something to eat. This mother was obviously suffering. She wasn't a torturer! She was unhappy about her son's fate, but she, unfortunately, didn't see any other solution for Christian, whose words were incoherent and who scared the whole village.

I released Christian, who was very quiet.

His mother apologetically explained his story: "He was a brilliant young man. We invested money from family, neighbors, and cousins to send him to study mathematics at the university in Bordeaux.

But he got the disease there. He worked so much that he became depressed and could not pass the test. The doctor in France sent him back here and said that he needed to rest. He came back, but he had changed. We no longer recognized our Christian. He was so obsessed by his failure that he hardly got out of bed. He was depressed and talked to himself. We had him undergo medical treatment and see a psychiatrist and some marabouts and healers, but nothing worked. It was as if he was broken on the inside."

This young man I was bringing back to Bouaké was indeed listless. He talked to himself incoherently in the back seat. I dropped him off at the center, showed him the dormitory, and explained: "We need you here. You're young and intelligent, and I think you'll be able to help us manage a center like this one!" He looked at me in disbelief.

In the next few weeks, I often visited Christian, who took his medicine and gradually came back to life. He very quickly opened himself up to the others and regained his self-confidence.

What did I do to bring about this change? Medically, nothing more than his family, who had him follow appropriate treatment, which was the one he was getting now. But I think that Christian experienced his returning to his family as a regression—a terrible failure. With the change of context, he regained his self-confidence and revealed the qualities he had always had—an iron will and a lot of empathy toward others. The broken man who had no future became a model: "the uncle" to whom the patients who had just arrived could entrust themselves.

In 2001, St. Camillus had four rehabilitation centers, including Dar-es-Salam, and we started to understand the patients better. Most of the time, their obviously irrational behavior, which often looked aggressive, was the fruit of their fear. Here's one example among a thousand.

I was on the road, a few miles from Bouaké, and I was going fast, as I often did, when I saw a man wandering. I recognized his hesitant walk and confused look. He obviously had a mental problem. I stopped my car a few yards away from him. I asked the bystanders if anyone knew him, but, since nobody could answer me, I offered to take him in my pickup truck to St. Camillus, where we'd look for his family.

He got into the truck without saying a word. He didn't look frightened, so this looked like an easy case to me. He sat next to me on the passenger seat, and we left in a hurry. I wasn't ahead of schedule, as was often the case!

The man was pleased with my challenging driving. He smiled and muttered: "Thanks for ... the truck." We made a rather sharp right turn when suddenly, the guy grabbed the steering wheel and pulled it toward him! The pickup truck ended up perpendicular to the road for a fraction of a second and then rolled over and finished its race in a ditch in a great clatter of sheet metal.

I was okay. I hurt everywhere, but I didn't think I had broken anything. I saw my passenger, whose head was bleeding, under me. My seat belt prevented me from falling on him. The truck was lying on its right side. I unbuckled my seat belt despite everything and pulled myself up through the window, which had shattered. This was a sad spectacle. The truck was doomed! But this wasn't the first or last one I had wrecked. And it didn't lose any gas. The motor was cut off. So my passenger could do no worse than what he already had. I was going to have a hard time getting him out of there, given his position. It was better for me to go find help.

I was bruised and left on the road in the opposite direction. When I returned with two men who had agreed to come help me, we noticed that the car was empty. We got back on the road when we heard some horns. I sensed a new catastrophe, so I ran toward the sounds. My passenger was in the middle of the road. He was running in front of cars, which were avoiding him as best they could! I ran to pursue him, and as soon as he saw me, he started escaping through the bush.

He could brag about having made me run. Luckily, he ended up stopping. I told him I didn't want to harm him at all, but he remained incredulous. "I smashed your car! You're going to kill me," he said, frightened. Then I talked to him at length to calm him down. He agreed to follow me after that. On the road back home, I asked him why he had pulled on the steering wheel, and he responded, "The curve was tough. I wanted to help." As for his throwing himself in front of cars later, he was obviously trying to kill himself because he was sure I was very angry with him and was going to kill him anyway. His strange behavior, which was hard to manage, didn't, as I thought about it, indicate any aggression.

This being said, since I've had this experience, I no longer take patients I don't know in the passenger seat. They go in the back. It's pointless to increase the risks of an accident.

AMIDOU

Amidou died overnight in the middle of a strange crater that he had dug around a tree. He was resting amid the tangle of roots that he had exposed—near his bowl of rice, which he hadn't touched. He was sick, but we didn't think it was so serious. In any case, Amidou was already rotten on the inside and "bewitched."

13

THE GREAT TEST

St. Camillus reached a critical size in 1998. Every day, I found new patients who entered the centers, and others left the centers. This became a small industry. We were supported by humanitarian organizations such as Fidesco. Some volunteers came to see us and helped us prepare medicine and food. They were surprised and sometimes frightened by our deprivation but were also impressed by our endeavors. They saw that former patients were actively involved in the association and became its pillars. During our "rounds," I brought some of them to release the sick Ivorians who were chained up in the bush.

Many associations offered to have me go to Europe, Italy, France, and Canada to testify to what the cognitively disabled people in West Africa were experiencing. When I traveled there, many of my contact people were flabbergasted. They thought that we in Africa had kept our families strong and that, consequently, we took care of our patients. But I also went to show our successes, which interested European caregivers. I must say that the conditions of mentally ill patients in Europe weren't good. I saw patients who were tied to their beds.

Their rooms were clean and sterilized, but they were just as imprisoned as our poor souls in their chains deep in the woods. What difference did this make for the patients? The patients in Europe were more commonly in a chemical straitjacket. There was no external problem, but these poor people were inhibited and rendered incapable of any progress or cure—more likely by abnormal doses of neuroleptics than by the hardest steel! St. Camillus's media coverage in Europe helped us bring in some substantial donations. On the other hand, I hoped that, at my humble level, I had participated in improving the perception of mental illness in Europe.

Yet the task to accomplish was still huge. When I returned from Côte d'Ivoire after one of these trips, I had barely landed in Abidjan when I had to take my truck back to Bouaké. I was worried. Léontine had warned me by telephone that there was no more medicine and that even the food supplies were starting to run out. I brought some medicine and supplies in my pickup truck, but they wouldn't last long. "God will provide." But there were moments, like the one I was experiencing, when we wanted to be assured of it! While I was thinking, my ear was listening to the voice of Soro Solo on the radio. This well-known journalist had a column called "The Grouch," in which he denounced the scandals that were linked to the condition of the country's administration.

"How was this possible?" he asked. "I was looking at the letter of a father whose child died. He had brought him to the hospital in Treichville, and the doctor requested an infusion for the child. The patients in our beautiful country have to buy their medicine themselves, so this father rushed to the pharmacy. But when he returned, the doctor was in a meeting. The on-call nurse refused to insert the infusion, and the child died. He died because the doctor couldn't be bothered during his meeting and because the pharmacist didn't take on the responsibility."

I turned the radio off. I was dismayed by what I was hearing. Poor Africa. I saw that St. Camillus seemed very small in the face of the immensity of this distress. It was in trouble. Even though we had four centers, this was no longer enough for our mentally ill patients: 1,044 were counting on us this year. In addition to this responsibility, we were supporting the prisoners and those who needed help with hospital operations.

It was time to limit the size of our association. I grabbed one of the phones I had in my pocket—for cell phones had arrived in Côte d'Ivoire—and I called my center managers one by one, while the road was bringing me closer to Bouaké. I told them: "We must limit the admissions. From now on, if a patient isn't tied up, leave him alone." I put my phone, which was still hot, back in my pocket. It seemed to weigh a ton. What I had just done broke my heart, but we had to stay within reason if I wanted this work to last.

I wasn't the only one that was thinking like this. In fact, for a long time, St. Camillus's active members had very gently tried to warn me. They told me it was time for St. Camillus to look to the future, to be able to make one-year plans, and to develop coherent budgets. So far, I was living in the present moment. Now, I had grown up, and St. Camillus had as well. I bitterly smiled at this thought. The nongovernmental organizations that had supported me had asked me for estimated budgets, and I was finally able to give them some numbers and indicate where every penny would be spent.

While I was thinking about this, I got a phone call. It was Esper Badi, my Lebanese friend, one of St. Camillus's great benefactors. He came along at just the right time. He was in the St. Camillus center with other members of the association and wanted to see me. I told him I'd be there in ten minutes.

After reaching Bouaké, I noticed a man who was walking oddly on the edge of the road. I started to examine him to see if he was one of the people who wandered on the streets and would need our help. But I changed my mind. No, there was no more room. He wasn't in chains. He didn't seem to be dying of hunger. So I left him and kept going.

I still had this heartache when I arrived in the center, where Badi was waiting for me. This man certainly won Heaven many times with all the services he rendered to us. He was a faithful friend and a true Christian. But he greeted me with a serious look on his face. Fr. Paolo and two French women who were helping us were there.

Badi asked me offhand, "Grégoire, do you want me to continue helping you financially?"

"Why do you ask? You very well know that we still need help!"

"I came here because I wanted an answer today. I need you to set St. Camillus's limits. You have to start organizing yourself."

I wanted to reply that I was starting to do it and that I saw that the situation couldn't continue like this. I understood Badi all too well! But I couldn't. At that instant, I felt I was directing St. Camillus on a very dangerous path.

After a moment, I lowered my head under the weight of the decision I had to make and heard myself answering him, "Badi, do you recall our first meeting? All that we undertook depended only on God—and you embodied God. Everything would have collapsed without your generosity at that time. God went through you, but tomorrow, He'll find another way to continue His work. Please, don't ask me to do what He didn't ask me to do. He didn't give me the task of organizing Him."

Before I started talking, I didn't how I was going to respond. I even thought of answering the other way around. But after having spoken, I realized I didn't need to change a word. Badi turned toward Fr. Paolo. "Did you hear that, Father?"

Father replied, "Yes, we must believe it. What he said wasn't coming from him. We really must believe it."

So Badi concluded, "In that case, I won't give you even five more francs."

After he pronounced his verdict, I heard one of the French women, who was devastated, sigh: "St. Camillus is ruined."

A little later, we gathered St. Camillus's managers together and told them: "Don't be afraid. If someone calls you because he has a sick person on his hands, go pick him up. Go on the streets and save those who are wandering."

I applied these daring words to myself and got back into my car for a trip in the opposite direction. It was a trip to the village of Mondoukou, on the Atlantic coast, which I had delayed for a long time. There I got in touch with Fr. Badéli, from the African Missions. He told me he had a lot of sick people on his hands, and he wasn't exaggerating. I made the rounds of the families and saw which ones needed help. From the very first visits, I could see that my pickup truck would be too small to bring everyone back. So I rented a bus. The vehicle didn't escape notice in Bouaké. As it passed by, St. Camillus's friends lamented: "Grégoire has gone mad!"

Yet even those in St. Camillus who disapproved of my behavior still did their utmost to serve the patients. They saw these lost people, who were sometimes scared, getting off the bus and were amazed that we were taking care of them and giving them shelter and hot meals. So nobody had the heart to blame me for having brought them back.

Luckily, we had more and more Western friends from Italy, Switzerland, France, and Canada who sent us money. Marco Bertoli, an Italian psychiatrist, joined the team as a member of the board of directors. We managed, with his help, to have St. Camillus recognized as a charity of the Church. In 1998, at the International Congress for Mental Health in Trieste, Italy, the St. Camillus

Association received the Franco Basaglia Prize for its fight against social exclusion. We had never dreamed of this, and it opened new doors for us to get help.

No sick person was abandoned to his fate. We set up our first center in my homeland in Benin at the end of the year. I'm now making regular rounds of conferences in Europe and Canada. It hasn't been very complicated. I've simply related St. Camillus's story, and I've seen that the hearts of those people, whose culture is different from mine, have been touched.

One year after my discussion with him, Esper Badi called me to make an appointment. I found my friend smiling and joyous. The shadow that had come between us was gone. He said to me:

"Grégoire, I wanted to see you to apologize."

"Excuse me, Badi, but apologize for what?"

"I saw God's action square in the face. St. Camillus doesn't come from you. This is obvious now. I thought I could make you give in with my money in order for you to be reasonable and in order for the association to be a long-term project. But when I retired, the opposite happened. St. Camillus did more without my help in one year than it had in all the preceding years!"

Thereupon, he gave me an enveloped that contained six hundred thousand CFA francs. This dear, faithful friend, who was God's instrument, offered me a lesson in humility and generosity. I have no doubt that he's in Paradise!

SÉVÉRINE

I was spread out on my mat and had been sick for so long that I had forgotten how it started. My life boiled down to a bowl of rice and a glass of water that I had from time to time and trips to the latrine, and that was all. I was nauseated and so tired that the least movement exhausted me. I had been a brilliant girl and had been preparing my doctoral thesis. But I was cursed. When I became tired, my village neighbors, uncles, and aunts came to warn me that Mama was trying to kill me. They said she was a witch. But I didn't understand why she was coming after me in this way. It's true that we had argued. She didn't want me to study what I was studying. But, for all that, did I deserve to die? I was sure that if we could meet, everything would become clear. But this was impossible. I didn't have the strength to get up or resist those who told me not to go see her.

14

PASSED THROUGH THE FIRE

By 2002, I was now the father of six children—five boys and a girl. They were doing well and, unlike me, were successful in school. With the centers that were multiplying and the business that continued to plague me, I was not home very much. But God takes care of us when we take care of Him.

One night, twelve of St. Camillus's managers, including me, met to pray together and review the association's situation. The centers were growing. Many of the patients had been able to leave the centers, although, unfortunately, some were relapsing and had to return there. Hélène took the time to read us a thank-you letter, which was written by a young man who had found a job after having gone through St. Camillus.

But some weren't so lucky. Baptiste, in particular, who came from Togo, didn't find anything, despite his training as a mechanic. This would have been unimaginable a few years ago. I knew him and was aware that he was doing everything he could to find a job. But there wasn't anything for him. Hélène spoke: "The problem is that Baptiste isn't Ivorian, and it has become harder for strangers to find a job." It was true that, with the economic crisis, Côte d'Ivoire was agitated by inter-ethnic tensions. So many Africans went there to work that a third of the country's residents weren't Ivorians—including my wife and me!

"Since the state coup in 1999, people have been suspicious. They prefer not to hire those who aren't part of their ethnic group," Hélène concluded. It was sad but true. Côte d'Ivoire had changed so much in one decade.

While I was thinking about this, my gaze lingered on the *Journal* that was spread out on the coffee table. It was turning into an unabashed xenophobic newspaper. "When Thieves, Homosexuals, Pedophiles, and Defilers Want to Appropriate Côte d'Ivoire" one headline read. The text was provoking: "In Côte d'Ivoire, some individuals with questionable morals, who are masters in the art of the denigration of our country and its institutions, are known as experts in pedophilia and homosexuality." By "some individuals," they meant northern Ivorians.

I don't want to talk too much about politics, but I have to give the setting anyway. After decades of Félix Houphouët-Boigny, who was president from Independence Day in 1960 to his death in 1993, the authority of Henri Konan Bédié, his successor, was contested. In order to oust Alassane Ouattara, his main opponent, Bédié introduced the concept of "being a true Ivorian." According to this concept, to be Ivorian and, thus, eligible to be president, one had to have four grandparents who were Ivorian. This wasn't the case for Ouattara, and so Bédié was elected president without any serious opposition in 1995.

The new president surely wasn't aware that, at that moment, he had opened a Pandora's box, for the situation in Côte d'Ivoire was currently fragile. The northern Ivorian Muslims were already suspected of not being good Ivorians.

Foreigners were scapegoated.... Bédié's strategy didn't work out for him. He was accused of corruption. The tensions between the north and the south increased. Then there was a coup in Abidjan. On December 24, 1999, Bédié was replaced by General Robert Guéï, who was nicknamed "Santa Claus in battle fatigues." He came to power with a simple program: "I'm going to make sweeping change, and then I'll organize some democratic elections."

Some presidential elections were organized the following year in difficult conditions that weren't very democratic. Many candidates, including Alassane Ouattara, were compulsorily eliminated, for they weren't considered "Ivorian" enough. In the end, the election appointed Laurent Gbagbo, but Guéï contested this result, and a conflict exploded. Gbagbo rapidly prevailed. The death toll from this violence at the end of 2000 was almost four hundred. This blood that was spilled in a country that had, up until then, been rather stable carried the seeds of what was to come, as we'll later see.

As the meeting came to an end, one of the participants warned us: "There are armed groups everywhere. The situation is out of control. We're expecting that, at any moment, there will be a new coup attempt." This Togolese man, a faithful member of the association, explained, "It is getting to be too dangerous to stay here. I have decided to leave Bouaké. I have to think about my wife and family. We are going to return to the countryside. I advise you to do the same. Things won't remain the same."

He was right. I saw that the country was edgy, and there were armed groups everywhere. It was becoming difficult to move because of the "road cutters" who improvised illegal "traps." The loyal security forces of Gbagbo's government were visibly overwhelmed. They wouldn't hold up against a serious incursion of rebels.

Yet another participant responded, "I understand those who want to leave. But I'll do what I can in order for St. Camillus to continue its work. Our friends are counting on us. I'll stay here."

This was also my position. Luckily, many of us shared it. St. Camillus had to face the storm!

The atmosphere was highly charged. I saw more and more Ivorians who were displaying weapons. Another sign, which was more subtle, but more worrisome for the future, was that everyone now knew who was a northern Ivorian and who was from Burkina Faso, Mali, Togo, or Benin. In the past, we didn't really ask any questions. The rich African and European foreigners left the country, feeling that the conflict could catch up with them. But we at St. Camillus were busy enough not to be too disturbed by these signs of a country that was preparing for a crisis.

While I was driving in Bouaké, I ran through our small trials in my mind. First of all, communication became harder. The roads were bad, and they became appalling. The frames of damaged cars blocked them. The improvised traps triggered giant traffic jams. This caused a cascade of negative consequences. Food prices soared. Many storekeepers were no longer supplied with gas.

For the remainder, there were still as many poor people who were left to themselves and needed our help. I was thinking about this when my vehicle was stopped by an unusual obstacle. A crowd of people, mostly women and children, who were loaded with bundles of every kind, were crossing the great "northern road" that connects Bouaké to Ferkessédougou. I stopped alongside one of the men who was carrying a big bag on his back and asked him, "Where are you all coming from? What's going on?"

"We're coming from the north. There are rebels everywhere. All the shops are closing, and we have nothing more to eat."

This was the eternal problem with wars in our country. As soon as things started to "heat up" somewhere, the whole population was thrown onto the roads. This wasn't so much because of the risk of dying under the bullets but because there was no longer any way to trade. The stores were no longer properly supplied, prices rose, and the situation became unbearable for all those—and there were many of them—who lived from day to day, without a penny to spare.

Bouaké became a city of refuge from one day to the next. But life also got complicated here. The price of food increased again. I had to go to Abidjan to buy enough reasonably priced food to feed people at home. Many friends told me to leave Bouaké, but I couldn't do it. There were too many people who needed me. At any rate, I still thought that the conflict might subside and that life would continue.

I was already at St. Camillus in the early morning of September 19, 2002. I was getting ready to take the car to go to Mass, but a young person warned me: "Don't go there! Don't leave. It's dangerous! The rebels arrived last night." I replied that I wasn't scared. After all, this wasn't the first time Côte d'Ivoire was shaken by political problems. So I climbed into my pickup truck and got going. I was happy with this day that was starting under a radiant sky.

My optimism subsided in the face of four heavy tree trunks lying across the road and barring the way to my daily Eucharist. Some very young people carrying weapons were standing behind the barricade. They looked suspicious.

I didn't know anything about weapons and safety regulations, but I was rather certain that holding a civilian at gunpoint, with your finger on the trigger, wasn't recommended. I had come across a band of overexcited rebels who were ordering me to get out of my car. They didn't have uniforms. Many of them were dressed in rags. On the other hand, their weapons seemed completely functional! While part of the group was holding me at gunpoint, others jumped into the back of the pickup truck and started to search it. There were rice and beans that I had reserved for one of the St. Camillus centers. I hoped the rebels weren't going to steal all that.

I was thinking about this when a very tall, thin rebel cried out: "Stop! Let him go. It's Grégoire!" I now recognized him. He was a prisoner.

I jokingly asked him: "What are you doing here? Were they crazy enough to let you leave the penal camp?"

He gave me a big smile. "No, the rebels opened the prisons. I'm with them now!" Then he spoke to the others: "I'm going to go with him so that there won't be any problem. Grégoire is with us!"

So I left again, with my tall passenger in the passenger seat. He beamed: "I'm really happy to be able to help you now! You know, everything is going to change in Côte d'Ivoire! It's going to get better!"

I asked him: "But what's going on? Was there a coup?"

He replied: "Yes, things could no longer go on as they were. But apparently, things didn't unfold as predicted in Abidjan. Luckily, the Ivorians don't yield in the face of tyranny here."

By questioning him, I understood that the country was now split in two. The loyalists held the southern part of the country—around Abidjan. The rebels held the north. They made Bouaké their capital. The future didn't seem as radiant to me as my new "bodyguard" promised. We went through deserted streets, which were simply haunted by groups of armed young people. We also passed in front of the Central Bank of West African States (BCEAO), whose windows were gutted. The rebels had apparently helped themselves to the glass.

But I was still able to go to Mass that day. My rice and beans arrived safe and sound. From that moment on, the rebels knew I wasn't an enemy.

Bouaké looked like a besieged city. Many of the stores no longer had anything to offer. On our end, we had been farsighted. We had enough rice to feed everyone for three months. Luckily, I had to leave for Spain and meet some of St. Camillus's partners. I had already planned large enough reserves so that there would be no need to worry while I was absent. Three months' worth was a lot, and, at the same time, it wasn't much, for who could say when we'd be able to return to Abidjan or Yamoussoukro to replenish our supplies?

I was thinking about this when I saw on the side of the road a lady surrounded by four young children. She was crying like a little girl, and her children didn't understand what was going on. I stopped and asked her: "What's the matter, my sister?"

She answered me with a sob: "My children are going to die of hunger. We no longer have anything."

I took them to the center, where I made a request: "Give them something to eat and some extra rice to take with them." With that, I went to see Cadi, who managed the warehouses, and told him: "We're going to organize a distribution. There are too many hungry people."

"But Grégoire, there will be nothing left for us," he responded.

I concluded: "God will take care of His poor people."

It was delightful to see mentally ill patients cooking and then distributing their dishes to "healthy people" in the midst of the misery of the war. The latter got in line in front of the St. Camillus center. The lady who diligently ladled hot rice into the bowls with a nice smile for each person had been wandering in rags in a wasteland in Bouaké a short time before.

While I was delighted about this magnificent scene, the manager inside me woke up. I knew this charity was costing us our reserves. I absolutely had to find a way to fill them! A crew from an Ivorian television station showed up at the distribution and filmed it in the face of the crowd that our initiative had drawn.

We kept going every day, and more and more people in the know were coming. A woman from the Swiss food program collared me during one of these distributions:

"What are you doing? This is crazy!"

"But, ma'am, people are hungry."

"You can't feed everyone!"

"God will take care of His poor people."

"What God?"

"Ma'am, leave me alone! Did I ask you to say anything?"

Thanks to the reporting, and thanks perhaps also to this lady who probably talked about our initiative to her organization, we received donations from everywhere. The Canadian embassy sent us two trucks with thirty-five tons of rice and cans of sardines and tomatoes. I had never seen this. Doctors Without Borders and the World Health Organization, which I had tried to contact in the past, came to help us to ensure our supply. There was only one problem to resolve. In order to obtain all these supplies of rice and fish, we had to go to Yamoussoukro or Abidjan—hence, to go from a zone that was held by rebels to one that was held by loyalists. Luckily, I started to know some people, so I could give it a try. I asked around for a truck. The first person who replied was Guillaume Soro, the leader of the rebels.[2] One of his emissaries came to see me and promised me a big truck that was in good shape. But I politely declined his offer. I wasn't supposed to take sides. Who knew what would happen tomorrow? If the rebels lost the game and we had made any concessions with them, what would

[2] Afterward, Guillaume Soro became prime minister. He was Alassane Ouattara's ally and ran for president against him in 2020. But his candidacy was invalidated by the Constitutional Council. In the end, Ouattara was elected to a third term with 94 percent of the vote. —Ed.

happen to St. Camillus? On a deeper political level, I didn't ask to know who was right. I had other things to do and a single focus: to preserve St. Camillus and take care of those who were abandoned.

I did well to refuse Soro's offer, for, in the end, it was the French army that found me a truck, in order for me to remove Westerners who were living in Bouaké and trying to get out of the conflict. I took two expatriate couples in the cabin with me. One was Italian, and the other one was French. They were going back to Europe. They were understandably very worried, for the hatred of the Ivorian extremists particularly affected the "white people" who were lumped together with colonizers. When we left, I was, as usual, forced to identify myself during the inevitable roadblocks that were set up by the rebels. Nobody gave me any trouble. Everyone knew me now. But during one of these stops, half a dozen rebels who were armed to the teeth stopped my vehicle. I sensed that my crew were keeping a low profile in their seats, for these guys didn't look very accommodating. Their chests were crossed with a strip of cartridges and a series of "bulletproof" charms that were supposed to protect you in a fight. The group's leader climbed on the step and asked me: "Are you going to the front line? Take us!"

It was hard to refuse. They climbed into the truck's dumpster with their weapons and bottles of alcohol. I heard them singing in the back when we got closer to the front line. I stopped the truck and told them: "After this turn, we risk meeting some loyalists. Get off here!" They didn't hesitate to do this and disappeared into the forest while continuing to sing.

I feared the worst for these young people or those who would meet them. They were kids, so to speak, with weapons that could send off the thirty bullets in their magazines in barely thirty seconds. These bullets could kill at a range of more than half a mile. Poor Africa. It only gets the worse from the modern era.

Shortly after setting off, I came across another roadblock, this one organized by the French army. The soldiers were participating in Operation Licome, which was supposed to separate the loyalists from the rebels. They were warned about my visit and took charge of the Westerners who had to leave. But they searched the truck's dumpster nevertheless. I heard a soldier say, "There's something in the back" and saw him get out a few moments later with another submachine gun, in addition to his weapon. One of the rebels had left it in the back!

I explained myself to the officer who was in charge of the road-block. He grimaced a little when he learned that I had driven some rebels, but he was supposed to be neutral. At any rate, he could see that I could hardly have forbidden them to get into my truck. He finally let me go by concluding: "You know, luckily, we are the ones who found it. If it had been the Ivorian loyalists, they could have accused you of arms trafficking and treason. This could have gone very badly for you and your passengers."

Yes, our guardian angels were watching over us, for I, of course, then had to go through many Ivorian loyalist roadblocks. Things got complicated when, on the way back, I had to go through loyalist roadblocks with my load of food. A furious officer castigated me: "It's with your rice that the rebels are fighting against us!"

"Excuse me, eh. Don't think that you're going to win with an embargo. The rebels aren't lacking anything. They are eating very well! Only the people are suffering!"

This was only too true. But if I had doubted God, I was wrong. I arrived in Bouaké with more rice, dried fish, and medicine than we had ever had.

SÉVÉRINE

I had left. I was in a center with former patients like me.
Mama wasn't a witch. Soon, she was going to see me here. I
seemed to be doing well. I could no longer manage to explain
to myself how I had sunk into this bottomless pit. Just a few
months ago, I had no longer seen any future. I was lost. I
only had one wish: to cry out to those who had experienced
the same thing as me and let them know that they could get
out of it. There's no curse powerful enough to bring down
a person who can rely on others and so regains his or her
confidence! I once saw a young girl who went through the
same thing I did—fear, lack of resources, and, above all, guilt
that consumes us from within. I hoped she could heal the
same way I did.

15

FIELD HOSPITAL

St. Camillus was now a meeting place in Bouaké that was well known to refugees and those who had lost everything, in addition to mentally ill patients, whom it was already feeding. The situation remained tense. Nobody knew exactly how the conflict was turning out. The loyalist media sank into xenophobia, and the rebellion was propagandizing.... Every morning, I expected that the fighting would close in on the capital. Yet, we had never been as well supplied with medicine as we were at this time! Thanks to the media attention that was set off by this conflict, nongovernmental organizations supplied us with all we needed for our patients. And these, for once, weren't second-class medicines or ones approaching their expiration dates.

In the early mornings, we saw some young men running with short strides on the streets and singing. These were often very young residents from Bouaké. They would make me smile, but the reality of the conflict caught up with me one morning when I saw a St. Camillus volunteer in tears. He told me that a rebel, "to practice shooting," had killed a mental patient who was wandering on the streets in Bouaké. It was, of course, impossible to find the culprit. And under which authority could I have him judged? We were floating in a legal vacuum. From that day on, we went through the streets to find the wandering mentally ill and bring them to shelter in our centers.

One morning in 2002, I realized that things were turning out even worse. My sleep was interrupted by the noise of automatic weapons. This sound was a part of daily life in Bouaké, with all these young armed people who couldn't help but play with their toys. But this time, the explosions were steadier. I was afraid the conflict was getting closer.

While I was on the road, I found that the rebel's usual roadblock was empty. I crossed it without any difficulty, but I saw some wandering dogs that were congesting the road. One of them obstinately stood in the middle. I blew my horn. The dog didn't react. Only when I drove toward it and threatened to crush it did the dog flee with its tail between its legs. Then I discovered that the dog had been eating a body. I stopped to see if there was anything I could do. I found that there were bodies everywhere. These dead people had been left at the mercy of the scavengers that were blocking the roads. They had bullet holes in them.

I got really angry. I said earlier that I had lost every notion of danger and have done things that were a little crazy three times in my life. This was the second time.

I got into my pickup truck and made the engine roar. I saw several groups of armed rebels wandering on the road, but I didn't pay attention to them. I didn't get any less angry. I had only one idea in my head. It was to see the one who was responsible for these massacres—the rebels' leader, who was lurking in the "headquarters" that they set up to the north of Bouaké. Those who were responsible for the New Forces (NF) were well entrenched. They brought together the Ivorian Popular Movement of the Great West (MPIGO), the Patriotic Movement of Côte d'Ivoire (MPCI), and the Movement for Justice and Peace (MJP). It was difficult to coordinate so many names that somehow brought together a multitude of small armed groups. Some concrete blocks reinforced by makeshift bunkers in front of the general headquarters forced vehicles to take a roundabout route to go in. But the sentinels let me go through when I screamed at them that I "wanted to see the leader." They were surprised at how angry I looked.

I burst into the middle of a general staff meeting. In the room were big, strong men in battle fatigues and a tall, burly man in their midst. The tall man was the rebels' leader. (Later, this man had a great career. As I'm writing these lines, he's now a colonel in Abidjan.) I shouted: "It's not going well, is it? You're murderers! The international community is watching you, you know! You're going to have the worst kind of trouble!"

The leader, who must have been almost two feet taller than I, looked at me defiantly. He was also furious. He replied: "You have a lot of nerve to come to my home to scold me as if I were a child!"

I immediately continued: "You say you're liberators, and you kill defenseless citizens everywhere? I could barely go on the road because there were so many bodies on it! Everywhere! Dogs were eating them!"

This time, the leader looked shocked. I saw that he didn't know how extensive the massacre was. I suddenly realized that I was in a dangerous situation. While I was thinking this, I heard some bursts of machine-gun fire very close by

The leader continued more quietly, with no concern for the explosions: "But you're scolding us because you love us. You're right to come see me if our security forces are overstepping their duties. I will personally see to it that these excesses stop!" The end of his speech was accompanied by a new "bang, bang, bang." I asked: "And these weapon noises—what's that about?"

This time, the leader smiled. "You see, Mr. Grégoire, this proves that I'm not telling you tales. We're now executing looters who were part of our ranks. A woman from Bouaké complained that they had robbed her. They admitted the facts, so we killed them. We don't have a prison, you understand, so we have to do justice with the means that are available to us."

Having arrived at this point in the conversation, I became aware, a little later, that nothing had prevented him from having me executed. I could have been eliminated just as surely as the poor guys who had just been sprayed with bullets. He need only have put a shovelful of sand over my body, and I would have simply disappeared. Nothing would have been easier. Nobody even knew I was there!

But my time hadn't come yet. He politely asked me to leave his house while promising that he'd take action to punish those who were responsible for the "excesses."

Luckily, these massacre scenes weren't repeated. But at the end of 2002, there was an atmosphere of death in Bouaké. Very few people drove anywhere because of a lack of gas. But I wasn't delighted to have the road all to myself. This war's atmosphere was weighing on me, and I was, at any rate, wasting almost as much time at roadblocks as I used to waste in traffic jams.

I spent another day driving. It was 9:00 p.m. when I finished unloading my truck in Abidjan. I liked to drive at night, for most of the time, the guards were too tired to be fussy. But when I reached a rebel zone at 2:00 a.m., I hit a snag. The rebel who had let me through on the way over said to me: "Too much. It's too much! You have a free pass, but you can't do any old thing! It's 2:00 a.m.

The curfew is at 10:00 p.m. You can't ride like this at any time! I'll take you to the general headquarters in Bouaké."

I answered him: "No problem. That's where I'm going. But can I go there with the truck? Look, it's full of food for the people in Bouaké, who need it."

The guy got angry and took me away, while one of his men drove the truck behind us. I suggested that they be careful with the truck, which the French army had lent us.

Arriving in Bouaké two hours later, they woke the leader up to decide on my fate.

He got out of bed, and his eyes were still drowsy. He told me: "Hello, Grégoire. So it's you again."

I responded very politely to him: "Hello, chief."

But the provocation over the roadblock interrupted our greetings: "This isn't allowed. Grégoire comes by at all hours — even in the middle of the night. He doesn't care about the curfew!"

The leader breathed deeply, looked at me defiantly, and said to me: "Grégoire, you know very well there's a curfew after 8:00 p.m. There's a war here! My men have been ordered to shoot at the vehicles that are moving around after 8:00 p.m. until daybreak. What you're doing is very dangerous."

I responded: "Well? Does the curfew concern me?"

The leader looked at me again. He seemed even more tired than before. He fell silent.

Then he turned toward the man who had brought me and said to him: "Listen, it's no longer necessary to bother me about Grégoire. When you see Grégoire, let him go."

I experienced a lot of peace after this episode. The roadblocks were lifted for me. The road was cleared of trunks and containers at the roadblocks that were held by the rebels. Thanks to that, St. Camillus's friends didn't suffer from hunger during the war.

But this war wreaked havoc elsewhere.

I had the privilege of rubbing shoulders with men from all the camps. They were familiar with my position. They knew that I spoke with everyone. My association with St. Camillus allowed me not to take sides. And then, I was from Benin, a small country that wasn't involved in the Ivorian conflict. Things would surely have been different if I had been from Burkina Faso. The Ivorian loyalists suspected that Burkina Faso's government was giving weapons to the rebels.

One day, my truck broke down in a loyalist zone, and while I was stopped there, a soldier came to me and said, "Grégoire, you must pray for me. My soul is lost." He was a nice young man from Côte d'Ivoire. He told me that his whole family was siding with the rebels. He stayed in the south and was convinced that Côte d'Ivoire's unity had to be preserved. But he had seen some horrible things. He told me they had rounded up people from Burkina Faso and made them dig holes. Then, when the holes were big enough, they put them at the bottom and buried them alive. "I couldn't do anything to prevent them from doing this," he cried. "Our leaders said that the people from Burkina Faso were killing us and giving weapons to our enemies."

I wanted to say that nobody could claim to wage a "clean war" — if that existed — during these Ivorian conflicts. A few years later, the press revealed that some rebels, who were followers of Guillaume Soro, had piled several dozen loyalists in a container and made them suffocate to death in the sun.

But even simple civilians who were staying away from the conflict could behave abominably. I didn't realize this until some poor people came knocking on St. Camillus's door in a pitiful state. They were dying, and their guts were on fire with acid that was gnawing at their bodies.

These were former prisoners from Bouaké's penal camp. Like all the others, they had been released when the rebels took possession of the city and opened up the prisons. But these people had the unfortunate idea of seeking refuge in the bush rather than joining the ranks of the rebels. They were starving and looked for help in a village. They were brought to the leader, but when the villagers discovered they were prisoners, they grabbed them and tied them up. They inserted pipes into their anuses and gave them an "enema" of acid. Once they were tortured in this way, they were abandoned at the bottom of the bush, still tied up, and left for dead. They managed to free themselves and joined us in Bouaké. They were writhing in pain. But we couldn't do anything for them. They died a few hours later. People don't want to hear about prisoners here in Africa. They are a disgrace for families, who prefer to leave them to their sad fate. There is no forgiveness for them.

JULIEN

Bam! Bam! We were clearing the tall grass to make room.
Mamadou, on my right, and Aristide, on my left, were vigor-
ously chopping it down with machetes. It was hot. We were
sweating, but we were joyous! We were going to plant yams
here. I had grown them about ten times in the village before
I got sick, so I supervised the operation.

I explained: "You really have to cut to the base. Then it
will be easier to dig in order to plant the rootstocks."

Mamadou began shouting with all his strength: "Plant
the rootstocks," which made Aristide laugh.

Mamadou had arrived for work several days ago. He
could scare people somewhat because he was about six and
a half feet tall, but he was kind and hardworking. I didn't
really understand what was wrong with him. He had bizarre
obsessions—particularly his annoying habit of repeating the
ends of sentences in his big voice, which carried. But what
a long way he had come! When he had arrived at the center
four weeks ago, he was living on another planet. He sat in a
corner and swung his head back and forth. Now he was an
active member of the group, even if he still had obsessions
and mostly repeated other people's sentences like a parrot.

"Mamadou! There's still a big trunk!"

"A big trunk" he repeated. Then the giant's eyes lit up, as
if he understood the meaning of the sentence by repeating it.

Since we had been clearing the ground, the tree trunks
we were uncovering were his little treat. We found out that
he loved to show how strong he was by pulling them out
with his big arms. The land clearers, in unison, put their
machetes down to see the artist at work. We formed a circle

around him while he was pulling on the tree trunk that was buried in the bushes. The comments were rife: "It wasn't necessary to disturb it for such a small piece of wood!" "It's hardly even a match!" "Yes, yes, it was worth it. He surely needs a toothpick!" Everyone laughed.

It was simple, and perhaps not very smart. But for many of us, these little moments of happiness were like being born again. Life began again. Soon, I would be able to go back home, where my daughter was waiting for me.

16

THE FIGHT RESUMED

January 2003. There was one more stop at a checkpoint. I didn't tell Francesco, who was occupying the passenger seat, but he slowed me down. He was an Italian journalist who wanted to go into a rebel zone. He had gotten into my truck in Abidjan at the same time as the rice and dried fish. It was a good thing that foreign journalists were interested in this crisis. I could see that since we had gotten media attention, it was much easier to get what we needed—especially food and medicine. But this had a cost. My white journalist drew my attention to all the gun carriers placed on the roads with the instruction to "regulate" traffic. We crossed the region that was being held by the rebels. This was already the third roadblock.

The guard asked me: "Why are you bringing a Frenchman with you?" The French didn't have a good reputation among some of the rebels, for the latter accused them of having prevented them from easily winning against the loyalists in September 2002.

The journalist responded by holding out his papers: "I'm not French. I'm an Italian journalist. I came to see what's happening in the rebel zone."

The other man, who was full of himself, attentively examined the papers and, after a while, responded, "That's good. In this way, you can show the loyalists that we're not murderers."

He wouldn't have stopped me without the journalist. But he was intrigued by a white man in these troubled times.

I had had enough of having to stop at all these roadblocks, and this trip from Abidjan to Bouké was long. I turned on the radio to listen to the news. This may seem strange, but I could wander around the whole country and was no more informed about the global situation than anyone else. I was familiar with some stories, but I had no idea what was going on in Côte d'Ivoire or what would happen to it. After some static, the voice of Radio France Internationale's (RFI) correspondent Jean Hélène came on. He spoke of upcoming peace agreements between the different parties that were going to be signed in Linas-Marcoussis, France.

Laughing, I said to my passenger, "You came too late. The war is over in Côte d'Ivoire."

He answered me, "I wish it were true, but I don't believe it."

"Me neither."

No, how could you believe that the war was going to stop overnight, while both camps were persuaded that their victory was stolen from them? This war saddened me and tired me out. After we arrived in Bouaké, we showed our credentials at yet another roadblock. It was the last one. St. Camillus was just beyond it.

But there was a new roadblock! I was annoyed and did something that was a little crazy. This was my third crazy action since my story started, if I'm counting correctly. I had my foot on the accelerator and threatened to crush the rebel who signaled me to stop. He scrammed, and we dashed off.

"Don't worry," I said to the journalist, who was a little taken aback. "I know him."

The truck was unloaded in record time at St. Camillus. There was already a line of people who moved forward with their bowls to get their hot rice.

Francesco whipped out his camera and started taking pictures. I saw in the line some mothers who had good jobs but were reduced to asking for help to feed their household. The upside of this situation was that the people who weren't talking to each other and were separated by the walls that others were trying to build between the social classes came together. I fleetingly hoped that some of this brotherhood, which arose from common misfortune, would remain when peace returned.

It wasn't for the moment. I saw on the doorstep a mother who was waiting for me. She looked anxious. I asked that we be left alone. I was familiar with the discomfort she was showing and her way of avoiding my look while telling me about her situation. She had a sick child—a daughter whose name was Djessou. She had left her in the care of a prayer camp. After being driven out by the war in Bouaké, she discovered St. Camillus and had talked with former "patients" about these sinister prayer camps. She was frightened by the idea that her daughter would be detained in the conditions she had heard about. She wanted me to help her get her daughter back. She was ashamed, for even if she didn't know the whole picture, she was well aware that she had gotten rid of her sick daughter. Now that she saw that treatment was possible, she wanted St. Camillus to take care of Djessou.

A little while later, I got back into my car in the company of this woman. Two volunteers from St. Camillus accompanied us. They were only too happy for this opportunity to leave the city for a little while. The camp was in a rebel zone about sixty-two miles from Bouaké.

It looked like a big farm. Animals were wandering around all over the place. We were cordially welcomed by some young people who introduced themselves as the prayer camp's "supervising staff." When I asked where the patients were, the voice of an elderly man replied: "In the fields!"

At first, I didn't know what to think of this pastor who welcomed us from his wheelchair. There weren't any bound patients in his facility who were lined up like toy soldiers. That was already a lot. He made them work and asked nothing from those who dropped them off. After all, I myself asked patients to study or work, for I know how bad idleness is. But Djessou's mother wanted to see her daughter anyway, and we felt that this request annoyed the pastor.

He played for time: "Give us a moment. She's working in the kitchen."

"I'm going to call her."

"No!"

If her work conditions were bad, I preferred to see her with my own eyes. So I ran to the kitchen without further ado. Djessou's mother followed me closely, and the old pastor came behind us.

Djessou *was* working in the kitchen. She was thin, dirty, and distraught. The meal she was preparing looked like what we served to the prisoners in Bouaké! Her mother cried, took her by her arm, and whisked her away without saying anything. She ran by the pastor, who tried to stop us: "If she leaves here, she'll die!" It was as if her "treatment" in the house of prayer was essential for her. He was furious and called down curses upon us as Jonah did on the city of Nineveh.

But, in the end, we got back on the road, and lightning didn't strike us. Djessou fit right in at the St. Camillus Center, and I provided a place for her in the brand-new facility that was being planned at that time: a rehabilitation center reserved for women.

People could think that life began again in this status quo situation of armed peace. We were going to start to build this rehabilitation center, as agreed with city hall. But an unexpected development brought our initiative to a halt. When it was time for the workers to start construction, we discovered that the land was already partially occupied by a Koranic school and a mosque that were being built. This was another problem to manage. I dashed off to the prefecture to explain the situation and was rather sharply received.

"Listen Grégoire, I don't want to hear about religion. I didn't know that Muslims were occupying the land. So I'm going to divide it in two."

But this solution didn't suit me. I needed the whole plot to build a decent center.

There was another smaller plot that could be entrusted to the Muslims. So I offered this: "Mr. Prefect, we will rebuild the Koranic school at our expense on the other plot. You'll just need to regulate all that."

He smiled: "There's really no wiser solution than this. I'm going to invite the religious Muslim supervisors. We'll see how they receive your offer."

This was probably the only reasonable solution. After all, the Muslims had built their school without any authorization. But I knew this wasn't going to be easy. The war strained the situation between Christians and Muslims. In theory, they managed to get along with each other in Côte d'Ivoire as well as in Benin. There were many interfaith marriages—with Christians, Muslims, and animists. But the rhetoric of the loyalists, who talked about "Iviority" and put all the "northerners," and Muslims in particular, in the "enemy camp," threatened this traditional coexistence.

I was thinking about this when the Muslim group arrived at the prefecture in long white outfits. I wasn't optimistic. Our workers came to tell me that the stakes they had planted for their measurements had been knocked over and thrown away in the night. In fact, the emissaries didn't look very accommodating, and I couldn't decipher the expression in the leader's eyes. He was a bearded imam who was directing the group.

As they were melodramatically sitting and taking their time to signify their importance in the prefect's office, we heard only the steady whirring of the fan. Then the prefect started a conciliatory speech: "There are always problems. Nobody is happy about it. But we must find a solution here." The imam didn't flinch. His head was slightly lowered, and his face was in the shadow of his hat. Most of the men around him, who left him the place of honor, seemed to be his sons. They surrounded him like a Praetorian Guard that was devoted to its spiritual leader. The prefect continued: "So, Grégoire—here he is—from St. Camillus is actually offering a solution which seems fair to me. But I wanted to talk to you about it before adopting it."

After this was said, the imam raised his head and looked serious. He declared: "Before saying anything, I want to ask your forgiveness for the damage that has been perpetrated. The one who did this is like my son. I'm taking his mistake upon myself. But we didn't know we were dealing with St. Camillus. St. Camillus doesn't take religions into account. It takes care of the whole world! We all have members of our families here in Bouaké who have been helped by this association."

We quickly agreed. The Koranic school moved, and I kept my rehabilitation center for women, which was a project I was very attached to. As a sign of respect, I made sure that the center's chapel, rather than the cafeteria or dormitories, would be built on the site of the former mosque. St. Camillus's work increased, despite the continuing war.

LÉONIE

"You are here in an insane asylum. This is your place. You've always been crazy." This was another voice. Before, I would answer them that I wasn't crazy, that I had an illness, and that this illness was curable. Now I manage to ignore them. These voices are painful. They still throw me off balance at times. But at the moment, they have lost the tyrannical power they had exerted over me. When they talk to me, I pay as much attention to them as to flies. Flies are certainly annoying, but I'm no longer going to let myself be bothered by flies. I'm twenty years old. I'm an intelligent young woman. I'm soon going to go back to school. I still have a long way to go! It will surely be hard, but I think about it with a smile, for I regained my strength in the St. Camillus Center.

17

GO NORTH!

July 14, 2002, was a big day. We opened the St. Camillus center in Avrankou, in suburban Porto Novo, the capital of Benin. It was a new reception center in which we offered accommodations for men on one side and women on the other. Sewing courses were organized there, and soon the first printed fabrics would come out of there. We also worked on educating the people from Benin, as we had done for the Ivorians. A film had been produced by St. Camillus's friends that showed that mentally ill people aren't bewitched but can be cured. The film was shown in parishes.

This new center was the result of a job that was as thrilling as it was grueling. In the evening, after the celebration of its opening, I told my wife: "This time, we're here. We can stop growing now that we have the centers in Côte d'Ivoire and the one in Benin. We're going to consolidate what already exists. We barely have what we need in terms of caregivers, medicine, and food." She smiled at me without answering me. She was happy—like me—about the work that had been accomplished. Blessed be God, who gave me such a wife! A year ago, He gave us a new child—our sixth one—Nicole, who was sleeping.

I also was getting ready to sleep like a baby. This official opening was a dedication. St. Camillus was now an international association, which benefited from solid support in Europe and Canada. What we were doing was bearing a lot of fruit. I said a final prayer of thanksgiving.

It was dark when, suddenly, while I was still awake, I heard a voice: "Go north!" This was very curious. I was certain I hadn't dreamed it. I immediately associated this voice with the one that had forbidden me from killing myself several years earlier.

In the face of this command, I got up without thinking and went to the bathroom to wash myself. There, in front of the pail of water and the piece of soap, was my watch. It was three o'clock in the morning! I verified this and opened my drowsy eyes, but that was it. It was still the middle of the night. What was I doing standing there, while I should have been sleeping? Yet, as if it had been arranged, I didn't have anything important to do that day. I had simply planned to participate in the organization of the Avrankou center. So I could slip away. But why go north?

I went back to bed. This voice was absurd. But I could not close my eyes. I got restless, turned, and ended up involuntarily waking Léontine up.

"Okay," she yawned, "you don't think Nicole is enough to wake me up at night? What are you doing?"

"I have to leave."

"Leave where?"

"To the north."

"Where in the north? You don't know anyone there!"

"I don't quite understand myself. Sorry. I must go there. I'll come back tomorrow afternoon to get the medicine."

I had to go to the minister of health in Benin two days later. He was storing medicine that I needed for St. Camillus.

I now had a Toyota pickup truck. It started with a turn of the key. I took the road to Parakou, which was more than 186 miles to the north. It wasn't close. I'd get there after sunrise. It was dark as soon as I left suburban Cotonou. I could have just as well entered a space vacuum. There was no lighting and no other vehicles. I wasn't afraid of "road cutters." Not many people from Benin ventured out at night outside the cities.

I asked myself: "Jesus, what are You asking me to do? I've never been there. How will I know what I'm supposed to discover there?"

But I got my act together. Once again, I was trying to organize and plan, whereas I should have been surrendering to God. Hadn't I received an obvious sign from Him? Weren't the moon and stars shining brightly? I sang the eighth psalm: "When I look at thy heavens, the work of thy fingers, the moon and the stars which thou hast established; what is man that thou art mindful of him, and the son of man that thou dost care for him?" (vv. 3-4).

But I didn't see anything. My headlights were chasing away the stray dogs that were prowling the roads at night when suddenly my thinking was interrupted by flashing lights piercing the darkness before me. There had been an accident. I saw two dead bodies. The police were already on the premises.

"Lord, what are You making me see? I don't understand!"

I drove past the scene and continued with my song, which had a hard time getting around the lump in my throat: "Yet thou hast made him little less than God, and dost crown him with glory and honor. Thou hast given him dominion over the works of thy hands; thou hast put all things under his feet" (vv. 5-6).

The sky turned white as I proceeded on the bleak road, which was as empty as the surface of a distant planet. Then the universe changed. I passed one and then two trucks. The streets came to life. I arrived in Parakou after traveling nearly 250 miles. I stopped near the first church. The priest was there, and he agreed to talk to me in private. I started to explain to him:

"Father, I'm coming to represent St. Camillus. It's an association that takes care of the mentally ill."

"You mean crazy people?" the priest immediately replied.

"Crazy people": I didn't like them to be called that. The conversation had gotten off to a bad start, but I continued anyway: "Uh, if that's what you want to call them."

"What do you want? They're on the streets if you want to see them!"

I saw that this wasn't where I was supposed to go. There was nothing to expect from this priest for the time being. I asked him how to get to the only city that I was acquainted with north of Benin.

"So, perhaps you could show me the way to Djougou."

"Continue to the crossroads. People will show you the way."

I felt that I was unwelcome. So I left and was a little angry. After a kind person showed me the way to go, I reflected while I was driving.

It didn't do any good to move forward like this at random. I was going to speak to a priest from the African Missions. I knew many of them, and if I named one of them, that would help strike up a conversation.

I went into a new church in Djougou, where a priest kindly welcomed me. I asked if there was a priest from the African Missions, and he replied that there was one there but that he was gone and would return in five days. I wasn't going to wait five days! So I talked to that priest about the association, but he replied: "Listen, this sounds interesting. There are a lot of sick people on the streets, but I don't know you. How do you expect me to commit myself to someone I don't know?"

I then went back into my shabby car and continued my trip north. My only stop was at a gas station, where I asked for directions in a part of Benin that I wasn't familiar with. Despite the evidence of the calling I had received, I felt lonely and useless. I had been driving for almost fifteen hours! The day was waning when I saw the sign that said "Tanguiéta." For me, this sign represented the end of the road. It was one of Burkina Faso's last cities; Pendjari National Park and Burkina Faso were after it. In the midst of my thoughts, I perceived that this name looked familiar to me. Ah yes! Tanguiéta was where Brother Laurent, who helped us at St. Camillus, was from. He worked in the Saint-Jean-de-Dieu Hospital!

For the first time in a long time, I sensed that my trip made sense. I went to the hospital's secretariat and said: "Hello, I'd like to see Doctor Laurent. Is he here?"

"Yes, he works here, but he left this morning for Cotonou," the secretary replied.

I got angry: "What are You doing, Lord? Did You make me travel for nothing?"

The secretary, who was a bit taken aback, kindly asked me: "Have you come from far away, sir?"

"I came from Cotonou."

"Oh dear ... But wait! If you wish, the doctor's assistant is here. He'll surely agree to receive you."

A moment later, I knocked on that man's door. He recognized me as soon as I walked in.

"But who's this? Isn't this Grégoire from Bouaké? Oh, Lord, blessed be You!"

He explained the situation to me. Three months ago, a group of nuns came knocking at the door of the bishop in Natitingou to say that there had been too many problems with mentally ill people who were wandering on the streets and that a specialized association would need to take care of them because the hospitals didn't know how to do it the right way.

I told him about my adventure, and we came to an agreement. This was a providential sign!

We immediately called the bishop of Natitingou, but he was traveling. So we made do with Djougou's bishop. He answered the phone, and as soon as I introduced myself, he started laughing and could not stop! I put him on speakerphone so that Brother Laurent's assistant could hear him as well. He was just as surprised as I was.

When the bishop caught his breath, he managed to say, "Ah Grégoire. God is mysterious! His providence is great!"

"Excuse me, Monsignor. Do you know me?"

"I know you only too well! We saw the film that was made by St. Camillus and showed it to our parishioners. I had forgotten to mute the phone, and when you called me, I was actually talking to them about the problem of the mentally ill. Ah, His providence is really great!"

This is how my relationships with the dioceses north of Benin started. God didn't let me forget that everything was in His hands. Every time I tried to organize myself to settle down, He reminded me that He was the one who was building. Psalm 127:1 reminds us of this: "Unless the LORD builds the house, those who build it labor in vain. Unless the LORD watches over the city, the watchman stays awake in vain."

With the bishop's help, we moved the patients who needed help to our centers. Then, a few years after this complicated trip, the learning farm in Agoïta, near Bohicon, opened its doors and offered work to about fifty men who were all former patients. They cultivated corn, cassava, rice, banana trees, and oil palms.

Their work somewhat relieved the centers' dietary needs. This job let those who were working on this farm get back in shape before returning to their villages, after having learned new agricultural techniques such as composting and crop rotation.

DJOUGOU

My head was against the path. I heard nocturnal noises in the bush and squawking and rustling in the leaves. My head was aching; I put my hand on it to try to pinpoint where the pain was coming from. I felt a void where my right ear was supposed to be. What happened to my ear? No, nothing, sorry. I lost it several years ago in a fight. Nobody cared whether I had an ear or that I even existed. Who would worry about this old madman who was lying on the road in the middle of the night? I saw two bright spots in the total darkness. They were quickly getting closer, and when I realized they were the headlights of a car, I got a terrible shock.

"Poor old man, poor grandpa." I heard a voice that was kindly speaking to me. I opened an eye and heard a laugh.

"He's alive, Father! God is great!"

A man was standing above me who was benevolently speaking to me under his big black glasses. There was a very chubby priest next to him, and both of them got ready to carry me cautiously. They put me in the back of their car and left in a hurry.

When I woke up, I was in a hospital bed. Grégoire, the man who had picked me up, often came to see me. He told me I had to get better and that there were centers for people like me who had a brain disease. He also told me he was sorry that he'd run over me with his car. But I very well knew that it wasn't his fault; I had been sleeping on the road in the middle of the night.

People I didn't know often came to see me. They belonged to St. Camillus and told me I had to recover and that they would take care of me. But I wasn't going to make it. I was too old, I had wandered for too long, and I was too ill. But, in the very end, I understood that I was still a man.

18

TO THE WEST

I took off from the Abidjan airport again in 2008. This time, I didn't go to Europe, but to Washington, where I was expected to introduce St. Camillus to the United States. Marco Bertolli, the psychiatrist, who was seated next to me, told me about this trip, which opened up great prospects for St. Camillus. He explained: "We're going to have a series of meetings with people who are in charge of nongovernmental organizations. This could be a springboard to get support and funding. We are particularly expected at the headquarters of the World Bank in Washington. The people who will be listening to you don't know anything about the treatment of the mentally ill in Africa. I think your testimony will impress them a lot." I absentmindedly listened to him. I was already half asleep. I don't really like flying because of that; it puts me to sleep.

But Marco went on with his recommendations: "On the other hand, I have to tell you, even if it's not with joy in my heart: you must not talk about God at the World Bank."

I suddenly woke up: "You're not going to start as well! I was already asked not to do this in Europe and have never understood it. I never was able to do it. If I don't talk about God, about whom do I talk?"

My European hosts often asked me not to speak about God during such and such a conference. But I didn't prepare my conferences. I simply testified to my own story, so at some time or another, God's name was bound to creep into my presentation. I couldn't help it, and Marco had known it ever since we had worked together.

Yet he insisted: "I've never asked you this before, but this time, it's really important. Don't talk about God during the conference. It may harm St. Camillus."

I knew he was saying this for the good of our association. The West is so complicated! But his request disturbed me. Didn't Jesus ask us to give to Caesar what is Caesar's and to God what is God's? Nothing would have been possible without God. I had to bear witness to Him.

When the day of the conference arrived, I entered the gigantic glass and steel building that stood close to the White House. That city is made for men to feel small. The security measures to go into the World Bank's headquarters were even more draconian than at the airport. They wanted to prevent me from entering with the chain I was carrying in my suitcase. The chain had been used to fetter a sick person by the neck to a tree for several years. The chain was heavy and rusty. You would have thought it came out of a documentary on slavery and the triangular trade. Yet it had been used only two years before. I showed it during conferences to make the listeners aware of the reality that the mentally ill in our countries experienced. This visual always had quite an impact, and I liked that it awakened consciences.

But the security guards didn't want to let it go by. I told them, with Marco's help—for I didn't speak English—"Listen, this chain is part of my presentation. I need it. I even brought it to the Vatican. You're not going to refuse it here!"

Nothing doing.

Marco translated this for me: "The security guard says that we're not in the Vatican here and that we can't take the chain."

I had this translated to the security guard: "So you'll explain to the meeting's organizers that I was prevented from coming and that I'm going back."

That's what I did. Luckily, the security guard stopped me. In the end, I was allowed in with my chain.

When the conference was about to start and I was standing behind my lectern, adjusting my microphone to my height, Marco slipped me a piece of paper. Surprised, I unfolded it and read: "Remember, you must not talk about God here!" Then I said this prayer silently: "Listen, I can't talk about You here. You'll know how to talk about Yourself."

When the audience gathered, I started to recount St. Camillus's path. I explained the way we took care of the patients and how we got their foot in the door for their professional lives. I didn't hide our daily difficulties and the terrible fate that was usually reserved for cognitively disabled people in our West African countries. At this point in the story, I put the chain around my neck and told how we had removed it from a young man who was suffering from schizophrenia. That young man was in a rehabilitation center at the time and would probably soon be able to return to his village. Everyone was very attentive.

During the question-and-answer session, many Africans from distant countries, such as Kenya, told me that the situation I had described was similar to the one they knew at home. They were interested in our model, which was very encouraging.

But a white American man seemed to be taken aback. He asked me a series of questions that were translated for me: "Sir, I don't understand anything you're telling me," he said. After this strange icebreaker, he continued: "You're not a doctor, a priest, or a healer. What made you decide to take care of mentally ill patients?"

I smiled at these words and turned toward Marco: "Now, whom do I talk about?"

He signaled me to do what I wanted, and I replied: "You're right. I'm only a simple tire repairer. My vocation started with a very difficult ordeal that Jesus saved me from. After this experience, I saw a naked man who was rummaging in a trash can, and I realized that this man was Jesus—the one to whom I owed my gratitude. Everything started from there."

The man then continued: "But ... sir, you should have started your testimony there! It's the root. You don't understand what you're bringing here. This testimony is very important for those who are listening to you!"

He came to see me at the end of the conference to tell me that the testimony of faith that I'd brought was very precious for Christians and those at the door of the Church. While listening to him, I became aware that I, who had come to help the poor, could also help those who were looking for Jesus. Those were people I had never imagined helping in the rich but secularized West. God's gifts are made in this way. They multiply!

Later, during my trips in the West, the people I spoke to often came to see me at the end of a conference to tell me that my remarks reconciled them with the Christian faith. This wasn't the goal I was seeking. I was thinking, above all, of my patients. But seeing such faith produces good fruit, changes the way people look at things, and restores confidence in a Church that's losing momentum in many so-called developed countries. A man at Sainte Anne d'Auray in Brittany told me: "I had renounced my Christian heritage and no longer practiced it. But now, I'm going to return to Mass, for I see that the Church is still the Church." Another man, who had the same background—raised a Catholic and disappointed by the Church—told me he was going to have his children baptized, whereas he had always refused to do it before.

This is why I think it's good for my conversion story to be published. Beyond the interest for St. Camillus, which I hope will be better known and get more support, I think the story of my journey could help Christians who are trying to catch their breath.

CHRISTIAN

Here I was. I knew Bordeaux, where I had a studio apartment just for myself. I was in a huge dormitory with a mat for a bed and a little suitcase. There were all kinds of boarders around me. Some of them had nervous tics and seemed to be elsewhere. I really preferred this. I loved my family, but I could no longer stand having them look at me and making me feel my failure on the test.

While I was unpacking my suitcase, Grégoire came to see me. He checked to make sure that I was settled in and was doing well. I appreciated this attention, for I saw that he was a very busy man.

"Christian, I need your help."

"But, Mr. Grégoire, I'm ill, and—"

"I didn't ask you how you were. Listen, are you making sure to take your medicine?"

"Yes, but I was already taking them before, and it didn't change anything, and—"

"Excuse me, but I have some cases that are much more serious here. You're a very intelligent and educated boy, and I've just spoken to the center's nurse. She's overwhelmed and will need a hand. So let's go together to see how you can help her. Would you like to?"

19

DON'T LET YOUR GUARD DOWN

"Father Grégoire, when do you think we'll arrive?"

Sébastien, who was in the back seat, was getting impatient. He was twenty years old, but he was worse than a kid! He talked all the time and wouldn't sit still. I often had to scold him like a child. He got scared every time. He was quiet for a while but couldn't help talking again. So when I started to have enough, I mentally went through Sébastien's journey and smiled, despite my annoyance. He had had some nervous breakdowns that lasted a long time. He spent the years when his friends became adults remaining motionless in a corner. It was really quite normal that he always wanted to talk. He was making up for lost time.

Christian, who was in the passenger seat next to me, buried his head in his hands as if to say, "Oh no! It's starting again!"

I turned my smiling face toward him and told him: "Come on. You also talked a lot when you started to get better. I called you my car radio!"

All three of us laughed. Christian, who is studying to be a nurse, had been one of St. Camillus's faithful supporters after his recovery. He came to help me out a little, which was welcomed.

We were in the middle of setting up a reception and rehabilitation center in 2015 in Sokodé, which is north of Togo. My pickup truck was getting ready to enter the country. I managed to come very late at night, as I had during the war in Côte d'Ivoire. The security guards were less attentive. They were half asleep and didn't have the heart to cause us too many administrative headaches—in theory. For there … Oh no, I had to stop behind a long line of vehicles. It may have been the dark of night, but there were soldiers everywhere, and they were even more nervous than usual. With the Togolese elections coming up—and rumors about the validity of those elections—the soldiers were afraid of riots. Moreover, I was going to the north of the country, to a region that was known to be rebellious against governmental authority. I was obviously going to be careful not to mention this detail at the time of the inspection, which I thought would soon arrive.

We waited for the whole night. Luckily, both my passengers fell asleep, which saved me from Sébastien's monologues. The sky was becoming white when I was finally able to leave. It was around the time when I was supposed to arrive at Sokodé's center; there were still five hours to go on the road. I was worried. I often tried calling the center's manager, but he didn't answer.

Sébastien, who had woken up, continued: "I'm hungry, Father Grégoire! Weren't we supposed to stop at the motel?"

"I don't have five francs to take you to the motel! We have a long way to go. Take it easy because we haven't arrived yet. You only have to ask Christian for some dried bananas."

These dried bananas were my emergency food. I always had some in the car. They were nourishing and rather good, but I didn't know what a nutritionist would think about them.

"Uh, Father Grégoire, I ate the dried bananas." This time, it was Christian who was talking. He looked distressed.

"Do you all want me to die? We're not ready to build this center with a team like this!"

A phone was ringing somewhere in my multipocketed vest. Since I was now traveling in various African countries and in Europe, I had a lot of phones, with many SIM cards, as bundling them was cheaper. This was sometimes difficult to manage. The center was surely calling! I searched before finding the right one. I hastily asked Christian to hold on to the steering wheel. It was something I shouldn't have done because it was dangerous. Incidentally, I won't do it again.

While Christian was keeping the vehicle on a relatively straight course, I finally found the vibrating object:

"Hello?"

"Father Grégoire! I was taken to jail. You have to pick me up at the police station!"

"In jail? What did you do?"

"We went to pick up some patients, but the people in Sokodé got angry. They said we were taking them to vote for the government. They wanted to stone us to death!"

Okay. Jail. An African jail, in particular, isn't really a good place, but it's better than an angry crowd during a Togolese election.

"I'm going to come get you, but I'm late. Tell them that everything is in order and that we're an organization that's recognized by the Catholic Church. You haven't shown them the bishop's authorization yet?"

"But, Father Grégoire, haven't you received it?"

I quickly thought to myself. No, I didn't receive it. Why would I have received it? It should have been addressed to the center in Sokodé. I really had a lot of trouble making them understand that I couldn't consolidate everything and that they had to learn to stand on their own two feet. Okay. The bishop forgot. So I didn't have anything to prove that we were a humanitarian association. As for the center, it was built without authorization, as usual. Things got tougher. I didn't show my distress to the person I was speaking to. He was a nice guy who was about twenty years old and was certainly terrified at the idea of staying in jail for a long time.

"Don't be afraid. I have everything we need. We're going to get you out of there!"

I took the steering wheel again and jammed the accelerator.

"Father, we're still hungry," Sébastien insisted in the back.

The fuel light came on. The vehicle was also demanding its pittance! While I filled the tank again, I exasperatedly looked at the trucks that were continuing on their way.

"I don't like it when—"

"Wait, I know!" Sébastien interrupted me. "You don't like it when the trucks that you've already passed pass you by because of fuel. Father, you say it every time!"

Here I was rambling on and on. Christian took advantage of the pause to buy a bunch of bananas from a traveling salesperson. It was a great idea.

I got another call once we got back on the road to Sokodé. This time, it was from Benin. The Bohicon center was calling me to tell me they had picked up a new patient; his mother had dropped him off. I asked what his name was: Paul. But when I asked for clarification—his last name and where he came from—people didn't know how to respond. So, I had to remind the centers' managers firmly of a point that I often reiterated to them: "You must not admit someone like this without asking for as much information as possible about where he comes from and his family. We're all like chickens, you know. We could die from one day to the next. Imagine that this could happen to the patient that you've just admitted. What would you do? How would you be able to contact his family?"

I've had to fight perpetually in order for commonsense principles to be applied.

When I arrived in Sokodé, I went directly to the prefect to explain the situation to him. I took with me a priest who lived in the city and knew us and backed us up in order to support our process with his authority. Luckily, the prefect welcomed us almost immediately. I explained the situation to him, but he interrupted me.

"Wait, I don't understand anything. You're an association that picks up mentally ill people on the streets, and you take care of them. Is that what you're telling me?"

"Yes, that's right, and since we're new in northern Togo, people haven't understood our process. They've thought we had bad intentions!"

"Ah, yes. I can tell you they were furious. When we intervened to lock your guys up, we saved them from death. They were on the verge of being stoned! People said you were going to make them vote for the outgoing president!"

"Our guys? You mean to say you took all of the center's personnel?"

"Ah yes, for sure; otherwise they would have been massacred. People were furious. The elections are occurring right now, and people aren't joking! I didn't know you. You had no official existence—not even a building permit!"

"And the patients? Are they left to their own devices?"

"As far as I know. I imagine so, yes."

My God. I envisioned everything that could have happened in the absence of those personnel. We had to resolve this situation at all costs. We called the bishop, who confirmed that he supported our action, and the prefect was understanding from that moment on. He probably didn't want to have to deal with a few dozen patients without any point of reference or supervision.

But I thought that, more deeply, our work had touched him. He hastened to expand the number of managers in the new center in Sokodé. Thanks to his kindness, this crisis, which could have gone very badly, ended up well. The center's patients managed to get by without leaders. They took care of the meals and didn't particularly notice that they had been left without any supervision. The personnel were released within a few days, and the whole company could carry on.

The prefect honored us with his presence during the center's official opening. He never blamed us for having built without an official authorization.

CHRISTIAN

This time, that was it. I was part of the staff in the Department of Health in Benin. It was a confirmation of my nursing studies and how far I'd come. I occasionally returned to St. Camillus's centers to help Grégoire. There was still so much to do! I hoped my job would let me change things for the mentally ill. They would see, by rubbing shoulders with me, that these illnesses weren't fatal.

AFTERWORD

Grégoire was going fast. He had been driving for three hours this morning. We left Benin and were now not very far from Sokodé, to the north of Togo — that is to say, it was about a ten-hour drive. He didn't want to be relieved. "It puts me to sleep," he replied. In fact, I got a little numb in the passenger seat, despite the conversation.

He was about thirty years older than I and didn't look tired. Since I had been with Grégoire in his daily life, I knew it wasn't easy for the man to stay still to tell me his story. Luckily, he spent a lot of time behind the steering wheel in order to move from one center to the other and manage the various crises. I used these trips to make small talk with him and to understand what moved him, while he steered his pickup truck, which was loaded with medicine.

Our discussions were often interrupted by the ringing of his phones. He was called about everything. There were administrative concerns, problems with patients, and more mundane problems, which were theoretically easier to handle — as it happened, water pipeline problems in the Togo center that we were going to. I was afraid to see the weight that was resting on his shoulders, but I didn't let him see my fear. He was smiling and sang when he felt like it—especially the eighth psalm: "What is man that thou art mindful of him?"

This was a question he sometimes wearily asked, as if he were sharing the psalmist's inability to understand the human pettiness that hindered his mission. I saw him get angry in the face of a collaborator's lack of initiative and the lack of governmental help. He sometimes ended a call with a "good night" that signaled the height of his irritation. I hoped he'd never wish me a "good night"! No, surrendering to God wasn't easy for this man, who often chose not to make plans that were too remote.

The future of the mentally ill preoccupied him, especially because St. Camillus wasn't finished—far from it. He talked to me about a center that he envisioned for mentally ill patients who were also drug addicts. Since he had discovered that a patient had brought hashish into one of these centers, he was obligated to have all those who came in searched. "The problem is that a patient who brings drugs can contaminate others. Their situation makes them impressionable and so vulnerable!"

He talked to me at length about some of them. He revealed his worries about his protégés to me without using notes. He knew each story. He talked, among other people, about Causette, a very joyous seventeen-year-old who didn't let anyone know about her past illness. She cut and sowed pretty tailor-made clothes at the Calavi center. "Those who, like Causette, were ill when they were teenagers are fragile. They didn't have time to grow up normally, and they can be fooled." He sighed: "I don't think she's listening, but I tell her to be suspicious of those she'll meet when she leaves. A pretty woman like that can come across anyone."

How will the more than one thousand patients who are living in the centers in Togo, Benin, Burkina Faso, and Côte d'Ivoire be taken care of when Grégoire is no longer there for them? He was well aware that he'd need a successor—someone who would pick up the torch after him. He spoke to me about several possibilities, including some consecrated laypeople who were being considered to pick up the—heavy—torch.

I'd heard criticisms about the St. Camillus Association. They didn't have the required competence and equipment to take care of the cognitively disabled. But, having seen the centers in Benin and Togo, I don't understand those who make these criticisms. Yes, the association obviously functions as a system that requires people to fend for themselves. It lacks resources and training. This year, the government in Benin gave it, all in all, a bag of beans and a bag of rice for support. I went with Grégoire to the Department of Health in Benin, where he bought medicine. The boxes of pharmaceutical products, on which was written "store in a cool, dry place," were piled up under a sheet-metal roof in a wide-open shed. The shed was "cooled" by fans attached to the beams. The expiration dates were varied, within one month of each other, and Grégoire loaded these medications into the truck, for he had nothing better to offer his patients.

But St. Camillus refused to leave anyone by the roadside. Who could condemn the association for this approach? Without its work, there would have been even more bound sick people dying in hovels or shackled to trees, with no hope of being saved. Unfortunately, they still exist. In Togo, I saw a sixteen-year-old young man with marks from chains on his wrists. He had just been released. But the people who bind a sick person now know they are outside the law. This is very different from practices of the recent past.

Grégoire didn't have an easy job, and sharing his daily life allowed me to debunk misconceptions about people who have so clearly put their lives in the service of the gospel. They don't live in a kind of beatific peace—going through trials without suffering.

On the contrary, they may suffer more deeply, but they also experience joy more fully.

During this trip to Sokodé, I assessed the empathy Grégoire maintained toward the patients, after being at their service for so many years. Although we were expected and were very late and he was driving fast—as always—he noticed an older woman wandering on the roadside who looked lost. He stopped suddenly, got out of the vehicle, and started questioning the bystanders as to who she was and whether she had a family. Nobody seemed to know. He then turned to the lady and started talking to her, assuring her that we could offer her a place where she'd be taken care of. The priest who was traveling with us came as a support. But she was scared; she hardly responded, and then she fled. Some bystanders came to see what was going on. The situation was tense, for St. Camillus wasn't well known there, and we could have been accused of kidnapping people. The elderly lady took advantage of the confusion and disappeared.

When he was back behind the wheel, Grégoire sighed several times: "Poor old grandmother. It makes me feel sad. These people are constantly attacked. That's why they can't believe we want them to be well."

I hope this book will contribute to sharing this natural and common empathy, which often stumbles in the face of learning disabilities. Learning disabilities are a frightening reality. This is probably what explains why they're so poorly understood and treated. Since we put intelligence at the forefront, we more or less believe that people whose intelligence is diminished lose a part of their humanity. This is why they are so bothersome and why we often fear to interact with them.

So the St. Camillus experience proves that contact and trust save sick people! Sometimes patients who are properly treated in the hospital and don't show any signs of improvement are entrusted to St. Camillus. Once they arrive in one of the association's facilities, they literally come back to life. St. Camillus doesn't have better medical treatment than what a hospital offers, but it allows patients to find a community that welcomes them and gives them responsibilities.

This isn't, of course, about denying the reality of mental illness or the effectiveness of medicine. But mental illness is considerably aggravated by the social stigma that accompanies it. This is especially true in countries such as Benin and Togo, where witchcraft makes an impact. Some of those in the St. Camillus centers who were labeled "crazy" were, in fact, simply people who had suffered from nervous breakdowns. They returned to a normal life with support and minimal medical treatment.

Some big clouds were piling up while I was thinking about this. They promised one of those storms that explode in an instant in Western Africa. They darken the sun and make such abundant curtains of water fall that cars end up swimming as much as they drive. This powerful force of nature that knocks over steel bridges and guts paved roads probably has its share in Africans' fatalism. The vast majority of them believe in the presence of spirits and think that when a spirit has taken over someone, that person is lost. He's possessed. Grégoire often heard this about one of the mentally ill patients that he helped.

In light of the poverty that is rampant, especially in Benin and Togo, it could be very tempting to "let go." How do we take care of the mentally ill in a country where a victim of a road accident could be left for dead if he doesn't have the money to pay the hospital? You have to have an unwavering trust in God to act in this way. Grégoire started to do this thirty years ago—without training or knowledge. Many people thought he was a visionary, but his work offered results that interested psychiatrists from all over the world. It would seem strange to attribute his success to chance. Thus, we must believe that he was following a plan, even if it wasn't necessarily his own.

—Thomas Oswald

Considered "bewitched" or "dangerous," the mentally
ill see their pathologies aggravated by isolation.

The fifteen-year-old young man seen on the right of the
photo still has on his wrists the marks of the chains that
bound him. He is now released, and his family, who
had tied him up, are no longer afraid of him.

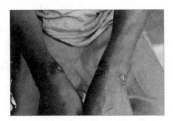

The rediscovered smile of Causette, who is perfecting
her art of sewing in a St. Camille training center.

Grégoire, always on the road, has a telephone in
each pocket. And he has lots of pockets.

These cooks prepare lunch for the 150 residents
of the Tokan center in Benin.

For Grégoire Ahongbonon, medical drug
supply is a constant concern.

An improvised dance at the Tokan center (Benin). Mutual aid, shared life, and common games are powerful therapies for the sick who arrive at one of the St. Camille centers.

The choir that sings in the chapel of the Sokodé center in Togo is exclusively composed of "patients."

Portraits taken at the Sokodé center in Togo.

Portraits taken at the Sokodé center in Togo.

Grégoire among "his friends" in front of the
chapel in the Sokodé center in Togo.

Sophia Institute

Sophia Institute is a nonprofit institution that seeks to nurture the spiritual, moral, and cultural life of souls and to spread the gospel of Christ in conformity with the authentic teachings of the Roman Catholic Church.

Sophia Institute Press fulfills this mission by offering translations, reprints, and new publications that afford readers a rich source of the enduring wisdom of mankind.

Sophia Institute also operates the popular online resource CatholicExchange.com. *Catholic Exchange* provides world news from a Catholic perspective as well as daily devotionals and articles that will help readers to grow in holiness and live a life consistent with the teachings of the Church.

In 2013, Sophia Institute launched Sophia Institute for Teachers to renew and rebuild Catholic culture through service to Catholic education. With the goal of nurturing the spiritual, moral, and cultural life of souls, and an abiding respect for the role and work of teachers, we strive to provide materials and programs that are at once enlightening to the mind and ennobling to the heart; faithful and complete, as well as useful and practical.

Sophia Institute gratefully recognizes the Solidarity Association for preserving and encouraging the growth of our apostolate over the course of many years. Without their generous and timely support, this book would not be in your hands.

www.SophiaInstitute.com
www.CatholicExchange.com
www.SophiaInstituteforTeachers.org

Sophia Institute Press is a registered trademark of Sophia Institute.
Sophia Institute is a tax-exempt institution as defined by the
Internal Revenue Code, Section 501(c)(3). Tax ID 22-2548708.